New D

Edited by Sally Welch   January–April 2016

New Daylight © BRF 2016

The Bible Reading Fellowship
15 The Chambers, Vineyard, Abingdon OX14 3FE
Tel: 01865 319700; Fax: 01865 319701
E-mail: enquiries@brf.org.uk; Website: www.brf.org.uk

ISBN 978 0 85746 386 9

Distributed in Australia by Mediacom Education Inc., PO Box 610, Unley, SA 5061.
Tel: 1800 811 311; Fax: 08 8297 8719;
E-mail: admin@mediacom.org.au
Available also from all good Christian bookshops in Australia.
For individual and group subscriptions in Australia:
Mrs Rosemary Morrall, PO Box W35, Wanniassa, ACT 2903.

Distributed in New Zealand by Scripture Union Wholesale, PO Box 760, Wellington
Tel: 04 385 0421; Fax: 04 384 3990; E-mail: suwholesale@clear.net.nz

Publications distributed to more than 60 countries

Printed by Gutenberg Press, Tarxien, Malta.

Suggestions for using New Daylight

Find a regular time and place, if possible, where you can read and pray undisturbed. Before you begin, take time to be still and perhaps use the BRF prayer. Then read the Bible passage slowly (try reading it aloud if you find it over-familiar), followed by the comment. You can also use *New Daylight* for group study and discussion, if you prefer.

The prayer or point for reflection can be a starting point for your own meditation and prayer. Many people like to keep a journal to record their thoughts about a Bible passage and items for prayer. In *New Daylight* we also note the Sundays and some special festivals from the Church calendar, to keep in step with the Christian year.

New Daylight and the Bible

New Daylight contributors use a range of Bible versions, and you will find a list of the versions used opposite, on page 2. You are welcome to use your own preferred version alongside the passage printed in the notes. This can be particularly helpful if the Bible text has been abridged.

New Daylight affirms that the whole of the Bible is God's revelation to us, and we should read, reflect on and learn from every part of both Old and New Testaments. Usually the printed comment presents a straightforward 'thought for the day', but sometimes it may also raise questions rather than simply providing answers, as we wrestle with some of the more difficult passages of Scripture.

New Daylight is also available in a deluxe edition (larger format). Visit your local Christian bookshop or contact the BRF office, who can also give details about a cassette version for the visually impaired. For a Braille edition, contact St John's Guild, Sovereign House, 12–14 Warwick Street, Coventry CV5 6ET.

Comment on New Daylight

To send feedback, you may email or write to BRF at the addresses shown opposite. If you would like your comment to be included on our website, please email connect@brf.org.uk. You can also Tweet to @brfonline, using the hashtag #brfconnect.

Writers in this issue

Sally Welch is a parish priest working in the Diocese of Oxford, working closely with families and young children. She is also Spirituality Adviser for the Diocese of Oxford.

Amanda Bloor is a Director of Ordinands in the Diocese of Oxford. She enjoys reading feminist theology and undertook research into how people develop priestly identities. In her spare time she is a chaplain to Oxfordshire Army Cadet Force.

John Twisleton is parish priest of Horsted Keynes in West Sussex. He is the author of *Using the Jesus Prayer* (BRF, 2014) and broadcasts regularly on Premier Christian Radio.

David Winter is retired from parish ministry. An honorary Canon of Christ Church, Oxford, he is well known as a writer and broadcaster. His most recent book for BRF is *At the End of the Day*.

Barbara Mosse is a retired Anglican priest with experience in various chaplaincies. A freelance lecturer and retreat giver, she is the author of *The Treasures of Darkness* (Canterbury Press, 2003), *Encircling the Christian Year* (BRF, 2012) and *Welcoming the Way of the Cross* (BRF, 2013).

Elizabeth Hoare is tutor in prayer and pastoral studies at Wycliffe Hall Oxford. A historian by training, she has a special interest in Celtic and desert spiritualities and a deep commitment to accompanying people in prayer. She is married to Toddy, an ordained Anglican priest and sculptor, and they have one son.

Andy John has been the Bishop of Bangor since 2008, having previously served all his ministry in the Diocese of St Davids. He is married to Caroline, who is also a deacon in the Church in Wales, and they have four children.

Lakshmi Jeffreys, as an Anglican priest, has served in parish ministry, university chaplaincy and as a mission officer across a diocese. She is now involved in church leadership in a village just outside Northampton.

Tony Horsfall is a freelance trainer and retreat leader based in Yorkshire, with his own ministry, Charis Training. He is an elder of Ackworth Community Church and has written several books for BRF, his latest being *Deep Calls to Deep*.

Sally Welch writes...

It is with a feeling of great privilege, and not a little apprehension, that I present to you this first edition of *New Daylight* with me as its editor. I am aware that I am following in the footsteps of some inspirational and creative writers and editors, so, as only the fourth person to undertake this role, I will do my best to live up to their example.

In this early part of the year, we follow the church in its regular pattern of penitence and celebration. The last few days of Christmas take us into the New Year with a look at times of feasting as they are shown in the Old Testament—both the uses and abuses of grand occasions, with fine food as well as ordinary meals that become celebrations as a result of the attitude towards the occasion of those who are present. These thoughts find their counterbalance in some reflections on times of famine, which were an ever-present threat in those times, and we find much to ponder in the management of such situations by some of our best-known Old Testament figures.

As we move into the still times of Lent, David Winter invites us to understand and appreciate silence, while, later, the drama and action of Jesus' Easter journey is shown to us through the eyes of Luke by Andy John. The time of celebration and resurrection joy that is the post-Easter season is mingled, for contemporary Christians, with the daunting realisation that we are now Christ's body on earth and we too must play our part in bringing nearer the kingdom of heaven. We are helped in this by the wisdom and love of Paul's letters to the Thessalonians, brought to life by Tony Horsfall. So it is that we are supported by the insights and knowledge of the *New Daylight* contributors as we continue our earthly journey together in the footsteps of Christ.

I am very proud to be able to contribute to the continuation of this special publication and hope that you will gain as much as I have from this edition.

Sally Ann Welch

The BRF Prayer

Almighty God,

you have taught us that your word is a lamp for our feet
and a light for our path. Help us, and all who prayerfully
read your word, to deepen our fellowship with you
and with each other through your love.
And in so doing may we come to know you more fully,
love you more truly, and follow more faithfully
in the steps of your son Jesus Christ, who lives and reigns
with you and the Holy Spirit, one God for evermore.

Amen

Lord will may not understand
you, but we trust you.

Feasting in the Old Testament

The Old Testament is an intricate book, with many themes and stories —some wide-ranging, others detailed explorations. Running through-out the wide range of poetry, history, narrative and prayer that we find in the Old Testament, like a golden thread of celebration and joy, are the descriptions of the feasts that were held by some of the most colourful characters we encounter.

The feasts were held for different purposes, but they all stemmed from the tradition of hospitality—one of the most important obligations of biblical communities. It was so important because, in the harsh desert landscape, where water was a precious commodity, to deny access to a well or watering hole was often to deny life. Similarly, to withhold food from a stranger who sought it might result in the death of that person and severe distress for the family unit that he or she had supported. Hospitality was, therefore, to be offered freely, in the expectation that the host in his or her turn would receive similar aid should it be required in the future. To deny hospitality was to threaten the very foundations of the desert communities, which struggled to survive on limited resources. In contrast to this, to offer lavish hospitality could demonstrate the hosts' wealth and power as well as their generosity.

Celebrations were incomplete without food. Meals held to com-memorate occasions in the shared history of a family or community served to bind together that social group even more closely, with addi-tional layers of shared memories each time such a feast was held. Feasting can be a religious act, too, in which thanksgiving is offered for the gifts of God, not only in the form of food and drink but also relation-ships, leisure and joy.

The following reflections begin by exploring the offering of food as part of the obligation of hospitality, even when the cost to the host is great, as well as the effect of denying such hospitality. I then look at some of the feasts that were occasions of celebration and a demonstration of power before examining some of the meals that were filled with sin and the consequences of those meals. Finally, I look with hope at the origins of the Christian feast we all share and look forward to those to come.

SALLY WELCH

Feasting as hospitality

The Lord appeared to Abraham by the oaks of Mamre, as he sat at the entrance of his tent in the heat of the day. He looked up and saw three men standing near him... Abraham hastened into the tent to Sarah and said, 'Make ready quickly three measures of choice flour, knead it, and make cakes.' Abraham ran to the herd, and took a calf, tender and good, and gave it to the servant, who hastened to prepare it. Then he took curds and milk and the calf that he had prepared, and set it before them; and he stood by them under the tree while they ate.

Abraham must have felt quite disturbed when he spotted three strangers in the distance, travelling at a time when the heat dictated a period of rest and stillness. Yet, in a land of scarce resources, the offer of water and food might save a life and would ensure the continuation of a practice that, in turn, could save the life of the host at a later date, in a different place. Additionally, it was held that to honour strangers was to honour God. This honour might be reciprocated by God showing kindness to the family of the host.

So it is that this elderly couple, disturbed from their habit of midday rest, do not shirk the responsibilities of hospitality placed on them by their God and their culture. They make a significant effort and expend time and scarce resources to welcome and nourish these guests. Perhaps in return, Sarah is promised the gift of a child—the thing she had longed for hopelessly for many years. Despite her disbelieving laughter at the news, Sarah does indeed bear a son, whom she calls Isaac, meaning 'he laughs', as a reminder of both her disbelief and her great joy.

Sometimes offering hospitality, particularly towards those whom we do not know well, can seem to be a trying burden. As Christians, we are urged to share what we have with others and, as the descendants of Abraham, we are reminded that, in honouring the stranger in our midst, we are honouring God.

Help us to remember that when we entertain others, we are entertaining God and his angels, and so to offer hospitality with grace and love.

SALLY WELCH

Food of angels: Elijah feasts

But [Elijah] himself went a day's journey into the wilderness, and came and sat down under a solitary broom tree. He asked that he might die: 'It is enough; now, O Lord, take away my life, for I am no better than my ancestors.' Then he lay down under the broom tree and fell asleep. Suddenly an angel touched him and said to him, 'Get up and eat.' He looked, and there at his head was a cake baked on hot stones, and a jar of water. He ate and drank, and lay down again. The angel of the Lord came a second time, touched him, and said, 'Get up and eat, otherwise the journey will be too much for you.' He got up, and ate and drank; then he went in the strength of that food for forty days and forty nights to Horeb the mount of God.

Elijah is weary and depressed. Jezebel, Ahab's wife, is furious that the priests of Baal have been executed on Elijah's orders and he has been forced to flee. In his moment of greatest triumph, when the power of God over the combined forces of the false prophets has been successfully demonstrated through the very person of Elijah himself, he cannot relax, for his task is still far from complete. It feels to him as if he has achieved nothing. The angel's appearance bearing food is a reminder of God's promise to Elijah that he will be with him throughout his life. Elijah may have lost hope, but God has not lost hope in him and this food is proof of that.

Sometimes even the smallest gift of food can be as nourishing and life-restoring as an entire feast. Given in the right spirit, with love and generosity, offered openly and wholeheartedly, a morsel of food can bring hope in a future. We see this not just in the effect of relief aid provided to famine-struck areas of the world but also in a box of chocolates that say 'thank you' to a neighbour, a celebration cake for a friend or a simple cup of tea and a biscuit to a weary or sad family member.

Help us to offer small acts of kindness to those around us, in memory of your great generosity to us.

SALLY WELCH

Hospitality as reward

At mealtime Boaz said to [Ruth], 'Come here, and eat some of this bread, and dip your morsel in the sour wine.' So she sat beside the reapers, and he heaped up for her some parched grain. She ate until she was satisfied, and she had some left over.

The young Moabite widow, Ruth, journeyed with her widowed mother-in-law, Naomi, back to Bethlehem, Naomi's birthplace. Conscientious and obedient, she rejected Naomi's instructions that she should stay in Moab and make a new life with another man and decided to share her future with the older woman, with whom she had become good friends. Arriving in Bethlehem, Ruth goes to glean the leftover grain in the field of a relative of Naomi's—the only source of food available to the childless widows—but Boaz, the owner of the field, has heard of Ruth's selfless actions and invites Ruth to share the meal of the reapers.

The meal Ruth shares seems strange—sour wine and parched grain—but it was a common repast for workers in the field with little time to spare for food preparation or cooking. The wine, often made from unripe grapes, would wash down the grain, made more digestible by being held in flames for a few minutes to break down the starches contained within. Although unpalatable to modern tastes, this meal satisfied Ruth's hunger and she would have returned to her task with renewed energy.

It is not the menu that is remarkable in this story, however, but the hospitality. Boaz' behaviour towards Ruth is daring, as Jews did not commonly share their meals with Gentiles; nor did men commonly share the same table as women. Boaz, however, is obeying a greater law—that of hospitality to a stranger, particularly to a poor widow with no male protector from whom she could receive support or aid.

Eventually Ruth and Boaz marry and it is through their great-grandson, David, and their ancestor, Abraham, that Matthew traces Christ's ancestry. Thus, an act of simple hospitality towards a poor stranger prepares the way for the incarnation.

The most basic hospitality, given with courtesy and thoughtfulness, can have an effect that is far beyond what we could imagine might come of it.

SALLY WELCH

Costly hospitality

Then the word of the Lord came to him, saying, 'Go now to Zarephath, which belongs to Sidon, and live there; for I have commanded a widow there to feed you.'... When he came to the gate of the town, a widow was there gathering sticks; he called to her and said, 'Bring me a little water in a vessel, so that I may drink.' As she was going to bring it, he called to her and said, 'Bring me a morsel of bread in your hand.' But she said, 'As the Lord your God lives, I have nothing baked, only a handful of meal in a jar, and a little oil in a jug; I am now gathering a couple of sticks, so that I may go home and prepare it for myself and my son, that we may eat it, and die.'

The obligation laid on the children of Israel by God towards the helpless and vulnerable of the community has existed since the great covenant Moses received on Mount Sinai and none was more vulnerable in those times than a widow. Yet, in a dramatic reversal of tradition, it is the widow who is called on to offer hospitality to the prophet, even though she has only extremely meagre supplies.

Trusting in the promise of Elijah that together they will survive this famine, she shares her final scraps of food with the wandering prophet—and her generosity is rewarded. Not only does her jug of oil never run dry, nor her jar of meal become empty, but also her son is brought back from the edge of death by the prayers of the man she took into her household as a guest.

This poignant tale acts as a reminder to us all that even the very poorest can reach out to those in need and the true heroes are not those who give a pittance out of plenty, but those who are willing to stretch what little they have to share with others. Then, indeed, a meal of bread and water can become a feast.

Let us not be so blinkered by tradition or expectation that we fail to notice those whom we can help, whatever our situation.

SALLY WELCH

Hospitality denied

One of the young men told Abigail, Nabal's wife, 'David sent messengers out of the wilderness to salute our master; and he shouted insults at them. Yet the men were very good to us, and we suffered no harm, and we never missed anything when we were in the fields, as long as we were with them; they were a wall to us both by night and by day, all the while we were with them keeping the sheep. Now therefore know this and consider what you should do…' Then Abigail hurried and took two hundred loaves, two skins of wine, five sheep ready dressed, five measures of parched grain, one hundred clusters of raisins, and two hundred cakes of figs. She loaded them on donkeys and said to her young men, 'Go on ahead of me; I am coming after you.'

It seems as if Abigail has exceeded the traditional rules of hospitality with the generosity of her offerings to David and his men as they seek sustenance after battle. Surely, the men did not need such luxurious and expensive foods? Abigail is not merely offering the usual level of hospitality, however, she is also trying desperately to make amends for her husband's gross lack of hospitality in the first instance. It is only right that she should do this as the safety of the community, which had been under the protection of David, is now threatened. Even Nabal's men feel the injustice of their master's actions and fear the consequences of denying hospitality that David had every right to expect. Fortunately, David accepts Abigail's offering and sends her away in peace.

God, however, does not allow the matter to rest there and, ten days later, we are told, the Lord strikes Nabal dead. On hearing the news, David woos the beautiful Abigail, who becomes his wife. Once again, the advantages of offering hospitality are demonstrated, as the generosity of a gift rebounds on its giver. The story of Nabal and Abigail does however make us aware of what happens when hospitality is denied to those who have a right to ask it of us.

Father of all, open our hearts and minds to the needs of others. Give us the grace to share freely, offering what we can to those who ask.

SALLY WELCH

Caught in the act

King Belshazzar made a great festival for a thousand of his lords... Under the influence of the wine, Belshazzar commanded that they bring in the vessels of gold and silver that his father Nebuchadnezzar had taken out of the temple in Jerusalem, so that the king and his lords, his wives, and his concubines might drink from them... Immediately the fingers of a human hand appeared and began writing on the plaster of the wall of the royal palace, next to the lampstand... Then King Belshazzar became greatly terrified and his face turned pale, and his lords were perplexed... That very night Belshazzar, the Chaldean king, was killed.

There is a famous painting by Rembrandt of this very moment when God's hand wrote its words of doom on Belshazzar's palace wall. The king is staring with horror as the consequences of his sacrilegious actions are spelt out while the rest of the diners look on in terror.

Under the influence of alcohol, Belshazzar has committed a foolish and sinful act and his punishment is immediate and severe. The king's death that very night reminds us that even at their weakest, as humiliated captives, God's people are being protected and his presence is with them. His actions are contrasted with those of Daniel, who regularly fasts and prays and remains detached from the debauchery of the palace.

The fate of Belshazzar highlights the consequences of inappropriate feasting, that overindulging in food and drink can lead to unwise or even harmful acts, for both ourselves and others. The story of the feast is a timely reminder that moderation is the wisest course to follow.

As we celebrate Epiphany, we remember the righteous obedience of the wise men, who honoured God and were rewarded with a glimpse of the Messiah. In so doing, we bring to an end the twelve feast days of Christmas. Feasts and celebrations are wonderful occasions and should be treasured, but we must be mindful that all good things come from God and must not be misused or abused.

Help us, good Lord, in the days ahead, to value, not abuse,
those gifts given to us.

SALLY WELCH

Political feasting

On the second day, as they were drinking wine, the king again said to Esther, 'What is your petition, Queen Esther? It shall be granted you. And what is your request? Even to the half of my kingdom, it shall be fulfilled.' Then Queen Esther answered, 'If I have won your favour, O king, and if it pleases the king, let my life be given me—that is my petition—and the lives of my people—that is my request. For we have been sold, I and my people, to be destroyed.'

The book of Esther tells of the bravery and wisdom of Esther, Xerxes' queen, who saved the Jewish people from a wicked plot to destroy them. The instigator of this plot, Haman, was jealous of Esther's uncle, Mordecai, and so planned to trick the king into ordering Mordecai's execution, after which the rest of the Jewish people would be slaughtered. Esther discovered his plan and, in a courageous and clever strategy, gambled on Xerxes' love for her that he would grant her wishes, despite the fact that she herself was Jewish. Amid great luxury and feasting, Haman's plot was revealed in all its evil and he was executed on the very scaffold he had designed for Mordecai.

The Jewish feast of Purim, instigated to commemorate this tale, is both a witness to Esther's faithfulness and a thanksgiving for the lives of those she saved by her actions. It is a celebration of goodness triumphing over evil, success emerging from potential disaster, joy born from apprehension. Special food is eaten, including *Hamantaschen*—little pockets of fruit-filled pastry, supposedly designed to look like Haman's hat. Gifts are exchanged and money donated to charity.

From a potentially tragic situation, a carefully orchestrated banquet reverses the fortunes of an entire people. It is only appropriate that the Purim festival should be energetically celebrated. We, too, should celebrate moments of triumph in our lives, times when disaster is averted, a success achieved or simply a crisis survived. No external agency is needed to grant us permission to throw a party. Whether it is a grand occasion or simply a small gathering of close friends and family, enjoy!

Set us free to celebrate and praise you for the deliverance you grant us.

SALLY WELCH

Feasting as celebration

When Joseph saw Benjamin with them, he said to the steward of his house, 'Bring the men into the house, and slaughter an animal and make ready, for the men are to dine with me at noon.'... Joseph hurried out, because he was overcome with affection for his brother, and he was about to weep. So he went into a private room and wept there. Then he washed his face and came out; and controlling himself he said, 'Serve the meal.'

This feast is an occasion that almost did not happen. A welcome meal is planned by Joseph, but he has been alone in a strange land for so long that when he finally sees his brothers all together, he is filled with emotion and has to leave the room. He soon recovers, however, and the meal continues, with much merriment.

The brothers are unaware that the feast is a celebration, for Joseph has not yet revealed his relationship to them, but it serves as an icebreaker, a way of reassuring the brothers that, while they are in Joseph's company, they will be treated as guests and not as hostages. It paves the way towards their full reconciliation with the brother they treated so cruelly, who has forgiven them fully.

The meal is also a personal prayer of thanksgiving on Joseph's part. Because Joseph remained faithful to God throughout long years of imprisonment and hard work, God, in return, has ensured the safety and survival of his family through the time of famine.

Our family celebrations, too, can include that extra dimension of praise and thanksgiving for the faithfulness of God to us and those we love. It is a faithfulness that endures through all things, even when they appear at their darkest and most challenging. As we, in turn, keep faith with our Creator, we will see God's hand in the events of our lives, in keeping with the covenant made with his children so many years ago.

Help us to be aware of your loving presence in our lives, that we may praise you in celebration of your faithfulness to us. May we remember and treasure your acts of loving kindness throughout our lives.

SALLY WELCH

A demonstration of joy

They brought in the ark of the Lord, and set it in its place, inside the tent that David had pitched for it... When David had finished offering the burnt-offerings and the offerings of well-being, he blessed the people in the name of the Lord of hosts, and distributed food among all the people, the whole multitude of Israel, both men and women, to each a cake of bread, a portion of meat, and a cake of raisins.

The lives of the people of England are punctuated by street parties, from those fuzzy black and white pictures of women and children eating jelly and cake from trestle tables at the end of World War I to the celebrations of the Queen's coronation, her Silver, Golden and Diamond Jubilees and various royal weddings. Indeed, street parties have become so popular that, in some areas, they are held almost annually, drawing communities together to celebrate events of significance and joy.

The story of David and the return of the ark of the covenant to Jerusalem is the tale of an Old Testament street party—an occasion that was so important to the people of Jerusalem, everyone had to share in it. The ark of the covenant was the precious container for the two tablets of stone inscribed with the ten commandments, given by God to Moses. A visible sign of God's promise to the children of Israel, that sign had been removed from them by the actions of Saul and had fallen into the hands of the Philistines, but the faith and courage of David had restored the city of Jerusalem to the Israelites and, finally, the ark to its true home.

David has a family of his own, a fine house with many servants and ample banqueting facilities, so he could have held a private celebration there, inviting just a handful of favoured generals and aides, but he does not do this. David wants everyone to share in the joyful triumph of this momentous occasion and, in a gesture of abandoned generosity, he distributes food to every member of the tribe of Israel, having first made that all-important offering to God.

Celebrations play an important part in the life of a community and we should endeavour to join in such occasions.

SALLY WELCH

Feasting as sinfulness

So when the woman saw that the tree was good for food, and that it was a delight for the eyes, and that the tree was to be desired to make one wise, she took of its fruit and ate; and she also gave some to her husband, who was with her, and he ate.

It was not much of a feast—simply some fruit picked from a tree—that Eve shared with her husband, but it marks the beginning of human-kind's rebellion against God and his ways. Adam and Eve succumbed to temptation and were punished, but they and humankind were not abandoned as God has kept trying patiently, again and again, to lead us gently back to the right path. Finally, he gave us his Son, who, by refus-ing to succumb, opened the path of salvation for all of us.

In addition, the consumption of the fruit of the forbidden tree is the story of our relationship with food more generally and the temptations that constantly assail us to damage and corrupt that relationship. The right amount of food, carefully chosen and prepared and eaten with awareness and gratitude, can make every meal a feast—an occasion for celebration, an opportunity for hospitality, a moment of thankfulness to the Creator whose bounty we share. However, to eat food that has been grown in ways that exploit people and environments, to eat food that damages the health of those who consume it or simply to eat too great a quantity of any food—these actions repeat that first sin of ingratitude and wrongful independence.

We have been given 'dominion over… every living thing that moves upon the earth' (Genesis 1:28) and it is our duty to be responsible stew-ards of God's creation. We can do this by choosing justly, preparing carefully and eating wisely of the abundance of good things that are available to us each day, aware of the God who created all life and asks us to play our part within his creation.

Father God, creator of all, help us to have right attitudes towards our food. Give us the grace to make every meal a feast, sharing what we have with others if possible, eating mindfully and gratefully, praising you for your great goodness towards us.

SALLY WELCH

Tempted by greed

Esau said to Jacob, 'Let me eat some of that red stuff, for I am famished!'... Jacob said, 'First sell me your birthright.' Esau said, 'I am about to die; of what use is a birthright to me?' Jacob said, 'Swear to me first.' So he swore to him, and sold his birthright to Jacob. Then Jacob gave Esau bread and lentil stew, and he ate and drank, and rose and went his way. Thus Esau despised his birthright.

The smell of a hot lentil stew, fragrant and spicy, must have been very tempting to Esau, hungry as he was from his hunting trip, but, as the elder son, his duties extended far beyond simply satisfying his appetite. Under Abrahamic law, Esau would become the head of the family on his father's death, inheriting the majority of his father's possessions and taking on himself the obligation for caring for the vulnerable members of the family. This was not a responsibility to be despised or taken lightly, but part of the fabric of the community, tightly binding it together with a web of mutual service. Esau allows his personal needs and interests to overcome his perception of his position within the bigger picture and, in doing so threatens the safety of his family.

We, too, must take care that our attitudes to the material things of life are not allowed to define who we are. We must be prepared to surrender our personal desires to the will of God. Our flawed and greedy natures must not corrupt our responsibilities as stewards of our environments and our obligation to honour our own bodies, not treating them with contempt by ignoring their need for healthy food, eaten in moderation and with respect to its origin. We can enjoy the gifts of God without becoming enslaved to them and can take care to share what we have with others without demanding more from them than they can reasonably or ethically give.

God of harvests and fruitfulness, we pray for the strength to withstand temptation and put the needs of others before ourselves. Help us to respect our bodies and honour their needs without giving in to greed.

SALLY WELCH

Feasting as a show of power

When the queen of Sheba heard of the fame of Solomon (fame due to the name of the Lord), she came to test him with hard questions... Solomon answered all her questions; there was nothing hidden from the king that he could not explain to her. When the queen of Sheba had observed all the wisdom of Solomon, the house that he had built, the food of his table, the seating of his officials, and the attendance of his servants, their clothing, his valets, and his burnt-offerings that he offered at the house of the Lord, there was no more spirit in her. So she said to the king, '... Blessed be the Lord your God, who has delighted in you and set you on the throne of Israel! Because the Lord loved Israel for ever, he has made you king to execute justice and righteousness.'

The arrival of an honoured guest is always an event. Houses are cleaned and made as tidy as possible, people are on their best behaviour and time is spent on careful preparation of tasty food. Solomon was no exception—the show he put on for the queen of Sheba was undoubtedly luxurious and elaborate. Indeed, the eventful meeting of two of the most powerful people of the time has been the subject of many paintings, musical compositions, books and films.

Although Solomon is rich and powerful and generous with his wealth, it is not because of this that news of his fame has reached the queen's ears. Solomon also has a reputation for being extremely wise and it is his wisdom that intrigues her. She arrives with 'hard questions' (v. 1) for him, questions he answers easily. It is this fact that finally draws her in to belief in the power and love of his God for his people, as he put such a man in power over them.

It is helpful to remember, when we are busy preparing for visitors, that, generous as our hospitality may be in material ways, the meeting of people is what lies at its heart.

God of wisdom and power, help us not to be distracted from
the true heart of hospitality by material concerns.

SALLY WELCH

Come to the feast

Ho, everyone who thirsts, come to the waters; and you that have no money, come, buy and eat! Come, buy wine and milk without money and without price. Why do you spend your money for that which is not bread, and your labour for that which does not satisfy? Listen carefully to me, and eat what is good, and delight yourselves in rich food.

As the Western world has become progressively richer, so the way we spend our money and time has changed. From each small community growing most of the food it ate, mechanisation and industrialisation have brought about a change in the scale of our food production. Food is now produced in huge amounts, often using impersonal and highly automatic methods. Many people living in cities are unaware of where their food comes from and with this lack of awareness comes a lack of consideration for the human beings and animals who produce it.

Westerners now need to spend a smaller proportion of their household income on food than in previous times and many have more to spend on things such as travel and leisure activities. One activity that has grown considerably in popularity is shopping—not just careful consideration of the things we need to buy, but as a pursuit in itself. This passage from Isaiah brings us back to the important issues and admonishes us to be aware that our priorities are the right ones.

Not only our bodily but also our mental health depends on food and we do need to be mindful of what we eat. Isaiah also uses food as a metaphor for our spiritual life. We should not be wasting our money and resources on those things that do not satisfy spiritually. Instead, we should be focusing our efforts on the wine and milk that is 'without price' (v. 1)—a relationship with our heavenly Father. These precious 'drinks' are available to us 'without money' (v. 1); all we need to do is accept the invitation that is held out to us by Jesus Christ. The 'rich food' (v. 2) of God's love will fill our hearts and minds and is offered in abundance to all who seek it.

Let us not become so focused on worldly things we ignore the spiritual feast that is eternally satisfying.

SALLY WELCH

Looking to the future

Tell the whole congregation of Israel that on the tenth of this month they are to take a lamb for each family, a lamb for each household... You shall keep it until the fourteenth day of this month; then the whole assembled congregation of Israel shall slaughter it at twilight. They shall take some of the blood and put it on the two doorposts and the lintel of the houses in which they eat it. They shall eat the lamb that same night; they shall eat it roasted over the fire with unleavened bread and bitter herbs... This is how you shall eat it: your loins girded, your sandals on your feet, and your staff in your hand; and you shall eat it hurriedly. It is the passover of the Lord.

The first Passover was a hurried, frightened affair. The blood of the slaughtered lamb was used to mark the houses of the children of Israel so that they might avoid the frightful punishment of God. The food was to be eaten as quickly as possible—it was a meal to sustain them for their long and demanding journey. There was nothing joyful or celebratory about this first Passover; it was a time of fear and darkness. God, however, led his people from captivity to freedom and the subsequent celebrations of this most auspicious occasion soon became filled with joy and thanksgiving.

The Passover is part of the Christian story, too, as it is the occasion on which Jesus gathered his disciples together for his final instructions in love and faith. That first Eucharist, celebrated in Jerusalem, echoes the simplicity of the first Passover, but is enfolded in love, as Jesus showed his companions how he was to be remembered. The shadows of death are to be found there also, but, just as the angel of death passes over the houses marked with the blood of the lamb, so Christ's sacrifice for us on the cross keeps us safe from harm and brings us the promise of a journey out of darkness into the promised land.

Almighty God, we give you thanks that, in your great love for us, you sent your Son to be our Saviour. Help us to celebrate his sacrifice with joy and hope as we travel with him towards eternal life.

SALLY WELCH

Minor characters in Genesis

'In the beginning'—these are the first words in the book of Genesis before God's creation of the heavens and the earth are described. From nothing, the 'formless void', the world as we know it comes into being and history begins. This and many other passages in Genesis are very well known—taught to us as children and serving to underpin our Christian faith: Adam and Eve's expulsion from paradise, Noah and the flood, Jacob's rivalry with his brother Esau, Joseph the dreamer and his coat of many colours. Alongside these major characters in big set-piece stories, however, are lesser-known men and women who often find themselves in difficult or challenging situations. They do not always behave wisely or well and their relationship with God can sometimes be erratic, but they all have tales to tell and should not be overlooked.

Genesis is all about beginnings—not just the beginning of the world itself but also the beginning of God's relationship with humanity and humanity's relationship with God. Each discovers—sometimes pain-fully—truths about the other. What does it mean to be human, to find your place in the world and live alongside others? How do we learn to care for creation, be responsible citizens and become aware that there are consequences to our actions? What might it mean to God to discover the way in which the freedoms given to humankind are abused or misunder-stood? How do we become God's people and how does the Creator choose to respond to humanity as our God?

The minor characters in Genesis remind us that, no matter what we are faced with, no matter how we react, God is with us. Through Christ, every day, every hour, can be a fresh start, a new beginning.

AMANDA BLOOR

Seth and Enosh

Adam knew his wife again, and she bore a son and named him Seth, for she said, 'God has appointed for me another child instead of Abel, because Cain killed him.' To Seth also a son was born, and he named him Enosh. At that time people began to invoke the name of the Lord.

If you have known someone who has lost a child, you will be aware that, for them, life can never be the same. A huge gap is left and the natural order of the world seems to be turned upside-down. It seems wrong for parents to outlive their children and to lose a child to violence, especially when that violence has been inflicted by a sibling, can seem the ultimate in cruelty.

The Bible does not describe how Adam and Eve reacted to the awful consequences of their sons' sibling rivalry. Instead, we hear, very factually, that Adam 'knew' Eve again and, as a result, she bore another son. I think it is significant that Eve does not refer to this new baby as a 'gift' or a 'blessing'; there is almost a sense of resignation that God has 'appointed' for her a replacement for Abel. It must have been hard for her to look at her new son without remembering the death of his older brother and hard, too, for Adam to bring up another baby, the first of many more. Life goes on, however, and I hope that some of their pain and loss was eased by the child they named Seth.

We know very little about Seth, but his birth matters. Seth lived to become a father himself and his firstborn son became the father of other sons and daughters. Cain steps out of the story and Abel died before he could have children, but Seth becomes the head of a family line that stretches, generations later, to another major figure in biblical history—Noah. For the first time in history, humanity has had to deal with death and has discovered that it is not the end.

Help us, O Lord, to not look back with regret, but look forward
in trust and hope.

AMANDA BLOOR

Shem, Ham and Japeth

God said to Noah, 'This is the sign of the covenant that I have established between me and all flesh that is on the earth.' The sons of Noah who went out of the ark were Shem, Ham, and Japheth. Ham was the father of Canaan. These three were the sons of Noah; and from these the whole earth was peopled.

Imagine, for months you have been sealed up in the ark and every living thing that was not shut away with you has died. God, tired of corruption and violence, has swept away the wicked and blotted out the past. All that exists are the wooden walls of your floating sanctuary, the animals that accompanied you and the members of your family. You wonder what is next. You wait as the rain stops, the waters subside and it is possible to step out on to dry land once more. Noah offers a sacrifice, God offers a covenant and—what next? Everything begins again and the whole world is your responsibility.

We know that Noah was a good man—that is why he was saved by God when the rest of the world was destroyed—but his wife, sons and their wives seem to have been protected by their association with him rather than because of any godliness of their own. We talk today, after major disasters, about 'survivor guilt' and I suspect that Noah's family might have found themselves asking why they were allowed to live when so many others died. Did they feel worthy? Were they able to trust God's promise that never again would the earth be destroyed? After all, a rainbow in the sky is little protection against the nightmares that visit you when you sleep, of hands reaching out of the flood waters, your friends and neighbours begging to be saved.

Yet, Shem, Ham and Japheth stepped out of the ark into a new life and their children and their children's children populated the whole of the earth. From that small group of survivors, bewildered and traumatised, the world began again.

Gracious God, remind us that if we step forward in faith,
you are there with us.

AMANDA BLOOR

Pharaoh and Sarai

When [Abram] was about to enter Egypt, he said to his wife Sarai, 'I know well that you are a woman beautiful in appearance; and when the Egyptians see you, they will say, "This is his wife"; then they will kill me, but they will let you live. Say you are my sister, so that it may go well with me because of you, and that my life may be spared on your account.'

Human trafficking is one of the major evils of our time. It is all too easy, in an age where travel is swift and human dignity often held cheap, for people to be treated as commodities and moved from one place to another for financial gain. Often the destination will involve prostitution or sexual slavery.

In this passage, we hear that beauty is dangerous. Abram knows that his young wife, Sarai, is desirable and he fears the consequences. He has little thought for her and she is given no choice in the matter; all that concerns Abram is that he survives. So Sarai loses the protection of being someone's wife and is presented to the Egyptians as his sister—single, available, marketable—and, as Abram suspected, she catches Pharaoh's eye.

The Bible says merely that 'she was taken into Pharaoh's house' (v. 15), but it is more than likely that this means Sarai was treated as one of his concubines. She has become a trafficked woman, moved from her home and given to another for gain. God rescues her, but the Sarah we meet later in the story has been changed by her experiences, becoming someone who laughs scornfully at the idea that she shall 'have pleasure' and the gift of a child (18:12). The man to whom she was bound in marriage put his own security above her well-being, and so Sarai has learned to view her beauty as a curse rather than a blessing.

God, however, sees Sarai as she is—a person, not a commodity. How do we, I wonder, view the victims of trafficking today?

We believe, Lord, that you know us through and through. Help us to recognise others as individuals who are known, loved and valued by you.

AMANDA BLOOR

Hagar

After Abram had lived for ten years in the land of Canaan, Sarai, Abram's wife, took Hagar the Egyptian, her slave-girl, and gave her to her husband Abram as a wife. He went in to Hagar, and she conceived; and when she saw that she had conceived, she looked with contempt on her mistress. Then Sarai said to Abram, 'May the wrong done to me be on you! I gave my slave-girl to your embrace, and when she saw that she had conceived, she looked on me with contempt. May the Lord judge between you and me!'

Psychology suggests that it is easy for us to put negative thoughts or impulses we may be having on to another person. So, perhaps we should not be surprised that Sarai, having suffered sexual exploitation herself, seems to have no sympathy for her slave-girl, Hagar, whom she places in a similar position. It appears that Sarai was given to Pharaoh by Abram and, in turn, Sarai gives Hagar to Abram in the hope that the slave will provide the child that Sarai has been unable to conceive. It is a cycle of abuse that can benefit no one.

Sarai desperately wants to have a child and offering her slave-girl as a surrogate is the only way she can see for Abram to have the heirs he has been promised by God (15:4). She might be afraid that Abram will set her aside and take another wife, leaving her once more defenceless and vulnerable. We do not know how Hagar feels about this arrangement—as a slave she had no choice but to obey the commands of her master and mistress and, perhaps, submitting to this arrangement offered her some hope of being given a higher status.

Hagar becomes pregnant and looks 'with contempt' (v. 5) on Sarai. Perhaps Sarai feels guilty, reminded uncomfortably of the similarities between Hagar and herself, for at last she seems able to recognise that she is angry with Abram, who, it would seem, let her down so badly in Egypt. It is Hagar, though, who suffers, as Sarai 'dealt harshly with her' and so Hagar ran away in fear into the desert (v. 6). Abuse has led to further abuse and suppressed anger has inflicted pain on another.

How often are we tempted to lash out at another, in angry or in pain?

AMANDA BLOOR

Lot's daughters

Lot went out of the door to the men, shut the door after him, and said, 'I beg you, my brothers, do not act so wickedly. Look, I have two daughters who have not known a man; let me bring them out to you, and do to them as you please; only do nothing to these men, for they have come under the shelter of my roof.' But they replied, 'Stand back!'

This is one of the most shocking tales in the Bible and it is hard to find any justification for Lot's actions. We can mutter about the duties of a host, about the exact meaning of the term to 'know', about cultural norms and the relative value in that society appointed to men and women, but the central message of the story remains. A father, faced with a crowd apparently determined on rape, offers them his virgin daughters to divert attention from the two men who are his guests for the night. This cannot and should not be explained away.

It is unclear why the men of Sodom were so determined to violate the visitors and the story does not suggest that Lot recognises them as the angels or messengers from God that they are later proved to be. It seems that Lot is a hospitable man, offering shelter and welcome to two travellers, which makes his willingness to sacrifice his daughters appear even more horrific in modern eyes, as he attempts to protect strangers at the expense of his own flesh and blood.

As elsewhere in Genesis, God intervenes, via the two visitors, to prevent harm occurring to innocent victims. Lot's daughters are saved from the potential repercussions of being handed over to the mob and Lot himself is saved from the consequences of such an action.

It is easy to see examples in the world of the violent mistreatment of others. It is all too easy to distance ourselves from the victims and perpetrators of such acts. If we believe that change is possible, we need to look the 'other' in the face. Each is an individual, known intimately by God.

God might ask us to sacrifice our own well-being, but can it ever be right to sacrifice others, even if it seems the right thing to do?

AMANDA BLOOR

Lot's wife

They said, 'Flee for your life; do not look back or stop anywhere in the Plain; flee to the hills, or else you will be consumed.'...Then the Lord rained on Sodom and Gomorrah sulphur and fire from the Lord out of heaven; and he overthrew those cities, and all the Plain, and all the inhabitants of the cities, and what grew on the ground. But Lot's wife, behind him, looked back, and she became a pillar of salt.

Just as Sodom and Gomorrah have become bywords for wickedness and sin, so Lot's wife has become a symbol of foolish regret. Despite the explicit warnings of the angels that Sodom and Gomorrah are to be destroyed by God and Lot's family must flee if they are to survive, Lot's wife lingers, looks back and is made 'a pillar of salt' (v. 26). Some will interpret the fate of Lot's wife as a punishment for disobedience. She was warned, but she chose not to listen to God and paid the price. Others may see this as a simple transaction of action and reaction. In looking back, Lot's wife lingered too long in a place where sulphur and fire were consuming two cities and she was herself caught up in the destruction.

I want to suggest a third possibility. In church life, it can be tempting to look back to a golden age when everything was better than it is now. Congregations were larger, sermons more erudite, finances adequate, communities more supportive. Energies can be depleted by fretting over the past: 'If only we could recapture what was, then we could be so much better now…' Instead, God asks us to move forward and promises to work with us in what is.

Perhaps Lot's wife stands as a warning to not waste our time looking backwards. She became calcified, a pillar of salt. Ours is a living faith, not a re-creation of our heritage or a museum of our histories.

Help us, O God of our ancestors and God of the future, to not hold on to what is past, but take what is good with us into new beginnings.

AMANDA BLOOR

Rebekah

[Rebekah's] brother and her mother said, 'Let the girl remain with us a while, at least ten days; after that she may go.' But he said to them, 'Do not delay me, since the Lord has made my journey successful; let me go, that I may go to my master.' They said, 'We will call the girl, and ask her.' And they called Rebekah, and said to her, 'Will you go with this man?' She said, 'I will.'

We have seen in other passages that it was commonplace for women to be treated as being subject to the oversight of others. Rather than being in control of their own affairs, fathers, brothers, husbands would make decisions for them. Here, however, we are presented with a woman who, although still dependent on the decisions made by the men in her family, is given a choice in the matter. As the events referred to in this story have been arranged by God's guidance, there is also an implication there, too, there is a choice—that, if she wishes, Rebekah can refuse to be part of God's plan.

Abraham has sent his servant on a journey to find a suitable wife for his son, Isaac. After prayer, the servant meets Rebekah at a well and identifies her as the woman suggested by God to carry on Abraham's line (vv. 2–20). Although the servant formally asks Rebekah's brother and mother for permission for her hand (v. 49), her family request time for her to think over the consequences of such an action. It is she who accepts the betrothal gifts offered by the servant (v. 22) and she who makes the decision to leave straight away. She has set her face towards a new future and is ready to take the first steps towards it.

Rebekah shows courage and determination, but there is a degree of impetuousness there, too. She does not know, when she first meets the stranger at the well, whom he serves. Perhaps that is why her family asks for ten days' grace before she leaves. Perhaps, too, it is a reminder that sometimes when God asks something of us the urging is too strong to delay.

Give us courage, O Lord, to respond to your calling, whatever that may be. Grant us the knowledge, too, that you offer us a choice.

AMANDA BLOOR

Abimelech, Ahuzzath and Phicol

Then Abimelech went to him from Gerar, with Ahuzzath his adviser and Phicol the commander of his army. Isaac said to them, 'Why have you come to me, seeing that you hate me and have sent me away from you?' They said, 'We see plainly that the Lord has been with you; so we say, let there be an oath between us and you, and let us make a covenant with you so that you will do us no harm, just as we have not touched you and have done you nothing but good and have sent you away in peace.'

Treaties, suspicion, promise and threat: it seems military and political strategy in Gerar was not too different from that we see happening in our world. The powerful men of the time—King Abimelech of the Philistines and his military and civil commanders, Ahuzzath and Phicol—are, to us, simply historical footnotes. To their subjects, they represented life and death, hope and despair, and the decisions they made would have affected the lives of all their citizens.

The disputes of the 21st century have largely been concerned with religious belief and economic prosperity. These are not new preoccupations. They can be seen in the interactions between Abimelech and Isaac, the son of Abraham, who settled in Gerar under God's guidance. Initially under the king's protection, Isaac became so prosperous and successful that he began to pose a threat (vv. 6, 13–14). If you are a king, you can afford to be generous to a stranger in need, but when that outsider grows to equal or overtake you in influence, the situation is very different.

The question of how to respond to migrants, refugees and asylum seekers is still relevant to Western society today. To Abimelech and his strategists, the faith practised by Isaac was crucial in their negotiations. It would be foolish to antagonise someone who appeared to be under God's protection, so they offered terms of peace—a promise to 'do… no harm' (v. 29). It was a simple solution, but, as often happens, it is not always easy to negotiate.

God of all the nations, teach us to look in others for signs of
your presence and work tirelessly for peace.

AMANDA BLOOR

Ephron the Hittite

Then [Jacob] charged them, saying to them, 'I am about to be gathered to my people. Bury me with my ancestors—in the cave in the field of Ephron the Hittite, in the cave in the field at Machpelah, near Mamre, in the land of Canaan, in the field that Abraham bought from Ephron the Hittite as a burial site. There Abraham and his wife Sarah were buried... and there I buried Leah—the field and the cave that is in it were purchased from the Hittites.'

I wonder if Ephron the Hittite had any idea, when he sold a piece of his land to Abraham, the 'stranger and... alien' residing in Canaan (23:4), that future generations would not only remember the transaction but also would be at odds over religious ownership of it? The reputed 'Tomb of the Patriarchs' stands today in the divided West Bank city of Hebron and is a site holy to both Judaism and Islam.

Ephron offered kindness to a foreigner when he agreed to sell the field, so that there would be a place for the remains of Sarah, Abraham's wife, to rest. It became the repository for Abraham's bones, too, and those of his daughter-in-law Leah. With each new interment, the pull of family loyalties to that particular spot would have become stronger. Yet this was land that was owned by one family but sat within territory belonging to another.

There has been an increasing tendency in the UK in recent years for small shrines to grow up at the spot where people have been killed in accidents. A bunch of flowers tied to a lamppost or a more permanent marker at a roadside or outside a building: these act as signs of regret and love and loss. What if a memorial becomes a disputed possession, though? How can that help to heal the hurts of bereavement?

Ephron would have given Abraham the land at no cost, but, by naming a price, he offered him dignity. God asks us to do the same and treat others fairly, even if we are in dispute with them.

Are there times in your life when you have held on to something physical—a possession, a place—because of what it signifies to you rather than what it is?

AMANDA BLOOR

Cured or healed? Luke the physician

Luke's two volumes set forth the trajectory of Jesus, starting with his acts in the flesh (Gospel) and then continuing after his death and resurrection by the Holy Spirit through his apostles and disciples (Acts). The volumes make up about a third of the New Testament and are compelling reading.

In the notes that follow, we will engage with the love, truth and empowerment of Jesus Christ presented by 'Doctor Luke'—an affectionate title that builds on Colossians 4:14, in which Paul describes his companion as 'Luke, the beloved physician'. Luke was neither an apostle of nor eyewitness of the earthly life of Jesus, but his fame stems from being a companion to Paul and his association with the third Gospel and the book of Acts.

The healing ministry, then and now, is part of the good news of Jesus as it breaks through bonds of sin, sickness, death and evil to bring us more fully into what we were made to be in God's praise and service. Luke's story of Jesus chronicles not just physical healing but also the healing from exclusion of lepers and the way in which Jesus includes social outcasts, as well as his ministering to women, which ran counter to the culture of his day.

The purpose of these notes is to help you welcome the power of God's word through the words of Luke into your varied situations. There is no word of God without power and it is the power to heal. As with Simon's mother-in-law (Luke 4:38–40), healing for us can be a call to helpfulness. The paralysed man who was lowered to Jesus through the ceiling (5:19–20) calls us to take more trouble to say healing prayers for sick friends. In the pages that follow, we will be reminded that faith is a gift of determination, bringing healing from fear (8:41–50) and entry into the wholeness of thankful living (17:15–19).

Healing is anarchic and hardly respects authority, save that of the God of life. It breathes joy and it has a forward momentum—the very trajectory Luke describes in his inspired writings as the good news of Jesus Christ.

JOHN TWISLETON

A man with an unclean spirit

In the synagogue there was a man who had the spirit of an unclean demon, and he cried out with a loud voice, 'Let us alone! What have you to do with us, Jesus of Nazareth? Have you come to destroy us? I know who you are, the Holy One of God.' But Jesus rebuked him, saying, 'Be silent, and come out of him!' When the demon had thrown him down before them, he came out of him without having done him any harm. They were all amazed and kept saying to one another, 'What kind of utterance is this? For with authority and power he commands the unclean spirits, and out they come!' And a report about him began to reach every place in the region.

When we pick up the Bible, we find both humanity and divinity. In Luke, we have someone expert in humanity with sympathetic powers of description, as in this passage, where the evangelist assures us that the demon exited the man 'without having done him any harm' (v. 35).

The unclean demon affirms the truth of Jesus' divinity, as others less attuned to the supernatural realm do so voluntarily later on in Luke's accounts. The demon is compelled to attempt to gain control and authority over his enemy by naming him. He loses out as Jesus has 'the name that is above every name' (Philippians 2:9).

Healing involves entering more fully into what we are meant to be in this world and the next. God sent 'Jesus of Nazareth… the Holy One of God' (Luke 4:34) to bring humanity into divinity so we mortals can 'escape from the corruption that is in the world… and… become participants of the divine nature' (2 Peter 1:4b).

Attaining the holiness associated with divinity is an escape from uncleanness. As the story of this man demonstrates, it is a divine action accompanied for most of us by a decided human endeavour that puts its trust in Jesus as Saviour and Lord.

Lord Jesus, by the power of your holy name, deliver me from the evil in my heart and bring me to wholeness of body, mind and spirit in the company of your holy ones. Amen

JOHN TWISLETON

Healings at Simon's house

After leaving the synagogue [Jesus] entered Simon's house. Now Simon's mother-in-law was suffering from a high fever, and they asked him about her. Then he stood over her and rebuked the fever, and it left her. Immediately she got up and began to serve them. As the sun was setting, all those who had any who were sick with various kinds of diseases brought them to him; and he laid his hands on each of them and cured them.

I know of several people who were brought into the orbit of St Giles, where I serve as priest, through the 'village lift' scheme. The helpfulness of church and community members in 'lifting' relatively immobilised people to the shops or to the doctors can sometimes lead them to find a place in the worshipping community. One lady recently confirmed was given lifts to chemotherapy during a period of freezing weather, and the helpfulness of one of our church members in so doing paved the way to her seeking the sacrament of anointing for healing. This, in turn, led to full Christian commitment and her own outgoing service in Jesus' name.

The story of Simon's mother-in-law is the other way round—one of healing leading to helpfulness. When God heals us, he does so for a purpose and not just for show, although some of the miracles of Jesus are astounding. This one is recorded by Luke as literally homely, as the lifting of a fever released the lady of the house to minister to her son-in-law's new companions, the disciples of Jesus.

Respecting the sabbath rules, Jesus waits until sunset before going to work, no doubt fortified by the good lady's cuisine, laying hands on 'any who were sick with various kinds of diseases' (v. 40). Luke tells us in a rather matter of fact way that he cured them all. The healing of so many must have added a good number of disciples to their group. We might imagine many being released that night into a servant ministry of helpfulness—that vital partner of healing in answer to prayer in the work of extending God's liberating reign.

Lord Jesus, make me an instrument of your purpose through both my prayers and my helpful acts.

JOHN TWISLETON

Jesus cleanses a leper

Once, when he was in one of the cities, there was a man covered with leprosy. When he saw Jesus, he bowed with his face to the ground and begged him, 'Lord, if you choose, you can make me clean.' Then Jesus stretched out his hand, touched him, and said, 'I do choose. Be made clean.' Immediately the leprosy left him.

Does God heal today? I would ask, rather, 'Does God change?' I am convinced that lack of expectancy in people's faith, concerning the possibility of divine healing, is a major impediment, even if there is a mystery about the process. It is always right that we approach God with both humility and confidence, as the leper did: 'Lord, if you choose, you can make me clean' (v. 12).

One of the debates in the healing ministry is over the need to qualify prayer for sick people with the phrase 'if it is your will'. Jesus' clear response to the leper's use of a similar phrase is a reflection of all that the Bible says about God's perfect will, which is to bring healing to individuals' bodies, minds and spirits and join them to the healing community he has called into being.

The outstretched hand and arm of Jesus reflect Old Testament imagery of God's arm being raised, at times in judgement, but also, as at the Red Sea, to bring about the salvation of his people. As a priest, I am privileged to raise my arms to bless and absolve with the authority of the Lord, whose ministry of reconciliation continues within the church.

In the passage, the leper seeks ritual cleansing—'you can make me clean' (v. 12)—as much as physical healing, as his condition bore with it the additional pain of exclusion from the worshipping community. Luke's Gospel describes an ongoing dynamic of healing and inclusion as the Lord favours segregated groups, the underprivileged, soldiers, women, the poor and well-known public sinners.

Here indeed is good news for today.

Father Damien of Molokai (1840–89), unlike his Lord, brought healing to lepers at the cost of becoming infected himself with Hansen's disease. He died, and was praised thereafter as a 'martyr of charity'.

JOHN TWISLETON

A paralysed man cured

Finding no way to bring [the paralysed man] in because of the crowd, they went up on the roof and let him down with his bed through the tiles into the middle of the crowd in front of Jesus. When he saw their faith, he said, 'Friend, your sins are forgiven you.'

I find intercession one of the most troublesome aspects of prayer. Maybe it is because it takes me so out of myself on behalf of others that I suffer an internal force of opposition. It may be a dynamic of the kind expressed by Newton's third law, which states, 'For every action, there is an equal and opposite reaction.'

The friends of the paralysed man here were part of his salvation, and what they did is a great picture of intercession—the way we 'carry' other people to the Lord. The friends went to enormous trouble, well out of their comfort zone, climbing on to a house roof, making a hole big enough for their friend on his stretcher to pass through and then lowering him down to Jesus for healing. Their selflessness contrasts, in the full narrative (Luke 5:17–26), with the self-interest of the scribes and Pharisees who stood opposed to and then dismayed by Jesus' healing action.

'When he saw their faith, he said, "Friend, your sins are forgiven you"' (v. 20). The man's healing was linked to both his own repentance and the faith of his friends, eloquently expressed in the trouble they took to bring him to the front of the queue. In this graphic story, we are reminded of how, in Christianity, faith is something shared. Each one of us is given a part to play in carrying one another to God—at least in heart and mind, if not, as here, with such physical exertions.

Comparing Luke's account with the other Gospels, we note, as we might expect, that the Greek word he uses for 'paralysed' is the one most commonly used among doctors. So, Doctor Luke brings his own expertise to the telling of this inspiring story.

Lord Jesus Christ, look not on our sins but on the faith of your church and grant us the peace and unity of your kingdom. Amen

JOHN TWISLETON

Jesus raises the widow's son at Nain

When the Lord saw her, he had compassion for her and said to her, 'Do not weep.' Then he came forward and touched the bier, and the bearers stood still. And he said, 'Young man, I say to you, rise!' The dead man sat up and began to speak, and Jesus gave him to his mother.

The great poet and mystic Dante Alighieri (1265–1321) had an affection for Luke, whom he described as 'the scribe of Christ's gentleness'. This passage is one of many that illustrate exactly that as, in his compassion, here he addresses a profound human tragedy—that of a widow burying her only son.

One way to pray the scriptures is to follow an idea used by Ignatius Loyola (1491–1556), which is to imagine ourselves in the passage and allow Jesus to engage with us there, via his Spirit. On one occasion I was praying through this passage in church during my morning prayer, using Ignatius' method. My mother had come to stay with us, but we hadn't really engaged with one another. As I prayed, I was led to see myself as the young man, 'dead' to his mother, and Jesus taking me in hand and giving me to my mother. I returned from church with a new mission of care for her.

Healing is closely linked to both prayer and care. In seeking healing, we cannot seek it for others without also seeking it for ourselves. We can only give what we possess and God is kind in showing us bit by bit things and people we need to engage with more fully, as well as things and attitudes and, on occasion, people we need to loosen ourselves from. This is a process that is transformative for us and for those in our circle of attention.

The widow of Nain had lost all, but Jesus stood beside her. The same risen Lord Jesus is beside us today, by the power of his Spirit, ready to open up for us his possibilities, which exceed our asking or imagining.

Think of any deadening influences in your life and ask Jesus to touch them so that you can enter more fully the vitality of his risen life.

JOHN TWISLETON

39

A girl restored to life

There came a man named Jairus, a leader of the synagogue. He fell at Jesus' feet and begged him to come to his house, for he had an only daughter, about twelve years old, who was dying... While [Jesus] was still speaking, someone came from the leader's house to say, 'Your daughter is dead; do not trouble the teacher any longer.' When Jesus heard this, he replied, 'Do not fear. Only believe, and she will be saved.'

'Two men looked through prison bars: one saw mud and one saw stars' (Oscar Wilde).

Choice is vitalising. At least, it is when we make the right one! Jesus himself had chosen to address the very serious situation in Jairus' household: his daughter was dying. That choice set Jesus on a journey on which, as we will see in tomorrow's passage, he stopped for a purpose. In his choice to serve the twelve-year-old girl, he was distracted neither by the sick woman who stopped him nor by the news brought to Jairus of his daughter's death.

Our Lord invites those nearby to join him in the choice he has made regarding Jairus' daughter, saying to them, 'Do not fear. Only believe, and she will be saved' (v. 50).

In the church's ministry of healing, we are caught up in the overarching choice that Jesus made, of life over death. As his discernment of the need in Jairus' household came also to be owned by others and proved to be immune to distraction, so in our day his divine possibilities open up to those who have the eyes of faith. Such gifts of faith involve the determined choice to walk through uncertainty, with God beside us, to the place where he wants us to go.

Luke encourages his readers in every generation to discern these possibilities, take Jesus at his word and move persistently towards them. As we walk the walk of faith, impossible things are made possible, all to the glory of God. As an outcome, people enter into relationship with the one who brings both healing and salvation.

'Look to [the Lord], and be radiant' (Psalm 34:5).

JOHN TWISLETON

A woman healed

As he went, the crowds pressed in on him. Now there was a woman who had been suffering from haemorrhages for twelve years; and though she had spent all she had on physicians, no one could cure her. She came up behind him and touched the fringe of his clothes, and immediately her haemorrhage stopped.

Luke tells it as it was, as do the other Gospel writers. Each evangelist tells the unique story of Jesus in different ways to suit their various readerships, but their core agreement has about it what scholar J.B. Phillips called 'a ring of truth'. It is hard to see why this woman's healing is linked to that of Jairus' daughter, except that this is the way it actually happened.

It is fascinating, though, to note a literary device linking both stories. For all of the girl's twelve years of life, this woman has haemorrhaged. Both women's destinies are touched by God at the twelve-year mark, and the number twelve has a perfect ring to it. Further, Luke demonstrates, here and elsewhere, that Jesus challenged not just the particular ailments but also the exclusion of women generally.

The woman in the passage has spent all her money. Sometimes the admission that we have no natural resources left prepares us to put faith in the supernatural power of God. The early years of my priestly ministry were spent among the indigenous people of Guyana in South America. Medical provision was uneven in the rainforest, so our weekly healing services were popular. Again and again, I saw bouts of malaria lift swiftly after a laying on of hands.

God is willing to touch with his healing all who approach him with humility and confidence in his provision, which goes right beyond our wildest imagining.

Pass me not, O gentle Saviour,
Hear my humble cry!
While on others thou art calling,
Do not pass me by!
Fanny Crosby (1868)

JOHN TWISLETON

Demons cast out of a boy

Jesus answered, 'You faithless and perverse generation, how much longer must I be with you and bear with you? Bring your son here.' While he was coming, the demon dashed him to the ground in convulsions. But Jesus rebuked the unclean spirit, healed the boy, and gave him back to his father. And all were astounded at the greatness of God.

The paradox of the scriptures is that their universal appeal is held in tension with cultural conditioning—here evident in the way that the symptoms of epilepsy are attributed to an unclean spirit. In his days in human form, Jesus engaged with a pessimistic view of the all-pervasive work of the devil, the author of demonic possession. At the same time, Jesus spoke clearly of our human dignity and responsibility, which puts the devil's work literally into the shade.

The unbelief that wearies Jesus in this passage concerns the devil's popularisation of untruth for, as Paul writes, 'Although everyone is a liar, let God be proved true' (Romans 3:4). What is not culturally conditioned is Christian faith in *diabolos*—literally, that there is an opponent of God's truth known as the 'father of lies'. He has just as great a power of persuasion in our day as he had 20 centuries ago. Although we now see epilepsy as a treatable physical sickness, it is folly to explain away or diminish the corrosive spiritual power of unbelief.

Luke's telling of this story is abbreviated compared to that in Matthew and Mark, so it comes to a climax in the sentence, 'All were astounded at the greatness of God' (9:43). In Jesus Christ, God's greatness, which diminishes fear of evil and affirms the sovereignty of good, is shown. In the account we read here, Jesus healed the boy and gave him back to his father.

Healing, with Jesus, is always an exercising of God's truth, power and love. Here, his truth confronts unbelief, his power counters disease and his love restores a son to his father.

'Let God rise up, let his enemies be scattered; let those who hate him flee before him' (Psalm 68:1).

JOHN TWISLETON

Jesus heals a crippled woman

Now he was teaching in one of the synagogues on the sabbath. And just then there appeared a woman with a spirit that had crippled her for eighteen years. She was bent over and was quite unable to stand up straight. When Jesus saw her, he called her over and said, 'Woman, you are set free from your ailment.' When he laid his hands on her, immediately she stood up straight and began praising God.

It was Pentecost and local churches had come together for a simple service of evening prayer followed by the laying on of hands. Jim was a tall man with a stoop on account of a back problem. After he had received the laying on of hands, he stood straight, to much acclaim, making for a memorable Whit Sunday.

The Lord Jesus, who laid hands on the sick during his ministry, continues to do so through his faithful followers, even if the healing process associated with those followers is less straightforward, due to our sinful shortcomings. His compassion for individuals is shown to be as sure today as it was for the crippled woman in the synagogue, who is described as receiving healing in today's passage. She was bent over and quite unable to stand up straight. Jesus spoke the word to her and then laid hands on her, providing a pattern for the church's healing ministry today—and 'immediately she stood up straight and began praising God' (v. 13).

When we meet Jesus, who is 'the same yesterday and today and for ever' (Hebrews 13:8b), things are straightened out—and not just physically. They say that 'God writes straight through crooked lines'—for example, in the way he blesses our bearing of affliction. The gospel also includes God's making 'crooked lines' straight, through, for example, physical healing in answer to prayer. Our ministry of healing is linked to the discernment of which of these two paths he has for us—bearing his cross of pain or being made to stand tall at his all-powerful touch.

'Surely he has borne our infirmities and carried our diseases; yet we accounted him stricken, struck down by God, and afflicted' (Isaiah 53:4).

JOHN TWISLETON

Jesus heals a man with dropsy

On one occasion when Jesus was going to the house of a leader of the Pharisees to eat a meal on the sabbath, they were watching him closely. Just then, in front of him, there was a man who had dropsy. And Jesus asked the lawyers and Pharisees, 'Is it lawful to cure people on the sabbath, or not?' But they were silent. So Jesus took him and healed him, and sent him away. Then he said to them, 'If one of you has a child or an ox that has fallen into a well, will you not immediately pull it out on a sabbath day?' And they could not reply to this.

This man had a very serious condition, known today as oedema, which is an abnormal accumulation of fluid beneath the skin between the cells in the body. Like many diseases, the symptoms of oedema point to causes that illustrate how the human body connects with its environs via, for example, diet. Therefore, relief from the disease has social and economic as well as medical aspects.

Doctor Luke's description of the healing of the man attends more to its social than its medical context—in particular, the destructive power of the legalism that Jesus confronted throughout his ministry. 'Let God be God,' he says; 'the sabbath is made for us and not vice versa.' His good news is a loosening of all that cramps the spacious life of God's children.

'If one of you has a child or an ox that has fallen into a well, will you not immediately pull it out on a sabbath day?' (v. 5). The King James Bible says 'ass' instead of 'child', but the NRSV uses earlier manuscripts and is probably right. Scholars pursuing this strange saying have identified a striking pun in the Aramaic language spoken by Jesus, where 'son', 'ox' and 'well' sound near enough the same. Humour of this kind is never far from the surface in the teaching of Jesus, who calls the Pharisees (and us, too!) to go beyond their superficial allegiance to the God of life.

'I came that they may have life, and have it abundantly' (John 10:10b).

JOHN TWISLETON

The thankful leper

Then one of [the ten lepers], when he saw that he was healed, turned back, praising God with a loud voice. He prostrated himself at Jesus' feet and thanked him. And he was a Samaritan. Then Jesus asked, 'Were not ten made clean? But the other nine, where are they? Was none of them found to return and give praise to God except this foreigner?' Then he said to him, 'Get up and go on your way; your faith has made you well.'

'Blow, blow, thou winter wind, thou art not so unkind as man's ingratitude' (Shakespeare, *As You Like It*, Act II, Scene 7).

Thanksgiving is at the heart of Christianity—so much so that the Greek word for it, *eucharist*, defines the focus of Christian worship. The word also appears in the story of the healing of ten lepers, related by Luke. It can also be seen as a parable, with many overtones.

The grateful man is a foreigner, and his gratitude makes for a vivid contrast with the evident presumption of his fellow lepers, who were probably from Jewish households.

There are echoes of the Old Testament figure Naaman the Syrian (2 Kings 5). Naaman was cured of leprosy after following Elisha's advice, and he, also a foreigner, returned to give thanks to the prophet for healing him.

Thanksgiving is a soil in which pride cannot take root. When we recognise profoundly that our lives come from, belong to and go to God, we possess the glorious freedom flavouring this story.

'Your faith has made you well,' says Jesus to the grateful Samaritan (v. 19). He is healed of more than just the social exclusion caused by leprosy. The walls of religious division have fallen around him through the gift of God. His spirit is imbued with a gratitude that will overflow into his future dealings.

Being made whole is a gift from God that comes through faith, impacting body, mind, spirit, social networks and, ultimately, the cosmos.

''Tis grace hath brought me safe thus far and grace will lead me home.'
'Amazing grace', John Newton (1779)

JOHN TWISLETON

Jesus heals a blind beggar

Jesus stood still and ordered the man to be brought to him; and when he came near, he asked him, 'What do you want me to do for you?' He said, 'Lord, let me see again.' Jesus said to him, 'Receive your sight; your faith has saved you.' Immediately he regained his sight and followed him, glorifying God; and all the people, when they saw it, praised God.

The 15th-century spiritual writer Ignatius Loyola had his feet on the ground when it came to saying his prayers. It was his practice to precede his daily meditation by voicing to God a request for the particular grace he was then seeking. That grace, in turn, he schooled himself to identify by imagining the question that Jesus asks in this passage being addressed directly to him.

'What do you want me to do for you?' (v. 41) Jesus says to each one of us. If only we can hear and answer him, our lives will be blessed and will be made more of a blessing to others. It is a searching question because it raises an even more demanding one—the question of what Jesus would want for us, which might be seen as our exact need at this moment in our lives.

'Lord, let me see again,' says the blind beggar. When Jesus replies, 'Receive your sight, your faith has saved you' (v. 42), he is given not just the ability to see physically but also to see Jesus. With that vision comes a cause that he is happy to throw himself into, heart and soul: 'he regained his sight and followed him, glorifying God' (v. 43).

Unbelief is pervasive in our materialistic culture that sets score on outward appearance to the detriment of what is on the inside. The prayer to see again is a prayer also for the opening of our inner eyes, which are faith's capacity to see God.

Listen to the Lord as he speaks to you in verse 41:
'What do you want me to do for you?'

JOHN TWISLETON

The sound of silence

There simply cannot be a stranger sentence in the whole of the Bible: 'There was silence in heaven for about half an hour' (Revelation 8:1).

It is not the 'silence' that is strange—though, in context, it is surprising—it is the 'half an hour'. How would you measure time in heaven, where time no longer exists? Eternity is not about length, but about quality and the reality of living with God. It is life as God, the eternal 'I am', knows it—the intensity of sheer being.

So, why 'half an hour'? Well, presumably, that was how the seer John measured it in earthly terms. It was not short, but it was not very long either and it was worth noting, for it was silence in the midst of both turmoil and glory.

This silence followed the opening of the first six seals (presumably the hidden purposes of God), a series of visions of the judgement of evil, then a magnificent vision of the heavenly throne room, where a vast congregation ('that no one could count', 7:9) was singing God's praises.

After that, the Lamb (Jesus) opened the seventh seal—and there was the silence. During that silence, the prayers of the saints were offered by an angel at the altar, with great clouds of incense rising to God, marking their offering of faith and love. Then the angel took the censer and hurled it down to earth. That was the end of the silence! 'Peals of thunder, rumblings, flashes of lightning and an earthquake' followed (8:5).

Over the next two weeks, we shall be looking at the way in which the Bible talks about silence. Life is noisy, turbulent, 'in your face', as we say. There are lovely sounds—a baby's gurgles, beautiful music, the sound of waves on a seashore—and there are, as Revelation so vividly reminds us, noises that are frightening, disturbing and terrifying. Then there is also this strange quality that we call 'silence'.

Silence is, as we shall see, so much more than simply the absence of noise. It is a positive quality, a grace, really—a very precious gift from God. Perhaps we, too, shall find that 'half an hour' is about right for creatures of time to seek it and find its gifts.

DAVID WINTER

The sabbath rest

Thus the heavens and the earth were finished, and all their multitude.
And on the seventh day God finished the work that he had done, and
he rested on the seventh day from all the work that he had done. So
God blessed the seventh day and hallowed it, because on it God rested
from all the work that he had done in creation.

These verses are, of course, the biblical authority for the sabbath—
probably the single most distinctive aspect of Jewish religious practice
all through the history of the religion. In the wonderful creation poem
of Genesis 1, the climax is the emergence of humankind, male and
female, made in God's image. God saw everything that he had made
and judged it 'very good' (1:31). Then, on the seventh day, he stopped.
That's the literal meaning of the word 'sabbath'—cessation. He did not,
of course, stop creating forever, but in this instance it was a kind of
celebration of work well done. God rested for a time and commanded
his human creatures to follow his example.

It was a principle that later became written into the very title deeds of
the Jewish faith and, subsequently, though it was applied to different
days of the week, of Christianity and Islam as well. However we choose
to see it, it is a creation principle. We toil; we rest. We are active; we
pause to restore our souls.

For the next two weeks, we shall be thinking about 'silence'. While
the sabbath and silence are not synonymous, the sabbath is emphatically
about the cessation of the bustle, stress and noise of the working week—
something the modern world has largely lost. Yet, the loving command
remains on the divine statute book, to turn aside from the pressures of
life and seek to hear the voice of God. To do so is indeed to practise the
sabbath, and be blessed.

*Sunday, too, is a 'celebration of work well done' as we give thanks for the
work of new creation through Jesus. We make space and silence
to be grateful.*

DAVID WINTER

Waiting in silence

For God alone my soul waits in silence; from him comes my salvation. He alone is my rock and my salvation, my fortress; I shall never be shaken... For God alone my soul waits in silence, for my hope is from him. He alone is my rock and my salvation, my fortress; I shall not be shaken. On God rests my deliverance and my honour; my mighty rock, my refuge is in God.

The temple worship of the Jews was certainly not silent, if the Psalms are any guide. Psalm 150 sounds as if it was very loud indeed, while Psalm 47 begins by telling worshippers to 'Clap your hands' and 'shout to God with loud songs of joy'. Yet here we have exactly the opposite— no clanging cymbals, tambourines or trumpets, but a call to wait for the Lord in the silence.

Perhaps the truth is that we need both—joyful exuberant worship and the silence of the attentive listener. We have a God who speaks, or there would be no law, no covenant promise, no gospel. In worship we praise him. In the silence of our quiet place we hear him. Nothing should be allowed to drown that voice. We make music for the Lord; we make silence for the Lord.

The psalmist listens for God alone in this silence. All other voices, sounds, distractions and concerns are excluded. That kind of silent attention is not easy in a world full of noise that includes lovely things, such as the noisy voices of our children coming home from school or nursery, the laughter of friends and neighbours, or even the sound of the church bells. In the midst of this noisy, energetic world, the call comes: 'for God alone my soul waits in silence' (v. 1).

To create our own little pool of silence—somewhere, somehow—is often the key to hearing his voice.

We listen in the silence for God alone, because he alone is our rock and our salvation, the strong foundation on which we build our lives and the source of our faith and hope.

DAVID WINTER

The waters of rest

The Lord is my shepherd, I shall not want. He makes me lie down in green pastures; he leads me beside still waters; he restores my soul. He leads me in right paths for his name's sake. Even though I walk through the darkest valley, I fear no evil; for you are with me; your rod and your staff—they comfort me. You prepare a table before me in the presence of my enemies; you anoint my head with oil; my cup overflows. Surely goodness and mercy shall follow me all the days of my life, and I shall dwell in the house of the Lord my whole life long.

Like many of the psalms, this one is an individual prayer rather than a collective act of worship. 'The Lord is my shepherd' is probably the best-known of all the psalms—many people know it by heart, and it is also available (as today's advertisements might say) in other versions. Yet, when we are considering the issue of silence in Christian spirituality, it may be overlooked.

In fact, this psalm is all about a believer's personal, intimate relationship with God. It is 'the Lord' (note the capital letters in your Bible) who is 'my shepherd', the great 'I Am', the eternal one, who leads me through life. He guides my path. He restores my soul. He brings me to rich pastures where I can be spiritually nourished. Thinking of silence, he leads me to 'still waters' or, more literally, the waters of rest. The picture is of a lakeside or smaller pool with a flock of sheep silently stooping to drink the refreshing water and, in the process, resting from the heat and constant journeying of the day. This is a kind of sheepy sabbath!

Even in the bleakest circumstances, the shepherd is there to lead his flock through the dark and deadly shadows. The relationship is intimate. Remember the words of Jesus, the good shepherd: 'I know my own and my own know me' (John 10:14). All the sheep have to do is listen, trust and follow.

'The sheep follow him because they know his voice' (John 10:4).
The voice is familiar because they hear it constantly.

DAVID WINTER

Do not fret

Commit your way to the Lord; trust in him, and he will act. He will make your vindication shine like the light, and the justice of your cause like the noonday. Be still before the Lord, and wait patiently for him; do not fret over those who prosper in their way, over those who carry out evil devices. Refrain from anger, and forsake wrath. Do not fret—it leads only to evil.

This is part of an unusual psalm, a kind of alphabetical guide to right living, possibly intended as a manual of preparation for young boys approaching their bar mitzvah. Each verse begins with the next letter of the Hebrew alphabet; needless to say, this gets lost in translation.

The section we are looking at today introduces an unexpected idea, signalled by an unexpected word: 'fret' (v. 7). 'Fretting,' it says, 'only leads to evil.' The English dictionary definition of fretting is 'to be constantly or visibly anxious', but the root of the word, both in English and Hebrew, carries the idea of something constantly wearing away at us—'fretwork'. When we are 'fretting' about something, it is gnawing at the back of our minds all the time. The example the psalmist gives is the insidious thought of people who have cheated or taken advantage of us—a nagging feeling of injustice, perhaps.

When we try to be silent in order to hear the voice of God, so often it is this fretting that worms its way into our thoughts. We seek to 'be still before the Lord and wait patiently for him' (v. 7), but the 'fret' keeps intruding. The psalmist suggests that, whatever its cause may be, trusting God is the remedy: 'trust in him, and he will act' (v. 5). God knows about it, whatever it is, and it can be left to him. Being still and waiting patiently for him is more profitable than fretting away about something that he can change but we cannot. Wise words!

To be still before the Lord may well require us first to identify anything we are fretting about—anything that may disturb the silence— and ask God to deal with it.

DAVID WINTER

The silence that speaks

The heavens are telling the glory of God; and the firmament proclaims his handiwork. Day to day pours forth speech, and night to night declares knowledge. There is no speech, nor are there words; their voice is not heard; yet their voice goes out through all the earth, and their words to the end of the world. In the heavens he has set a tent for the sun, which comes out like a bridegroom from his wedding canopy, and like a strong man runs its course with joy. Its rising is from the end of the heavens, and its circuit to the end of them; and nothing is hidden from its heat.

Perhaps some of you are already singing these words to Haydn's magnificent setting in his oratorio *The Creation*. The psalm is itself a glorious hymn to the Creator, but it goes beyond that. What he has made speaks to us, the psalmist says, even though space, sky, sun, day and night have no voices. Their eloquence, though silent, proclaims the glory of the Creator. This psalm is a call to listen to that silent voice.

Many of us love and enjoy nature. We find inspiration in the beauty of the sea and hills, birds and butterflies. In all of them we can recognise the hand of a God of beauty as well as power, but can we 'hear' the silent message of the 'wonder of his works'? The works themselves are speechless and voiceless: they cannot be heard with our physical ears, yet their words go out to the end of the world. They speak, as the poet Gerard Manley Hopkins says, of 'God's grandeur'. While we do not worship nature, we can and should let it speak to us of the majesty and beauty of the Creator. To see with the eye but not recognise his handiwork is to be deaf to his divine voice.

We stand on a seashore or a mountain top and are silenced by the beauty and majesty of what we see before us. That is the silence of the wordless message of the Creator. May our ears be tuned by the Holy Spirit to receive it.

DAVID WINTER

The stilling of the storms

For you have been a refuge to the poor, a refuge to the needy in their distress, a shelter from the rainstorm and a shade from the heat. When the blast of the ruthless was like a winter rainstorm, the noise of aliens like heat in a dry place, you subdued the heat with the shade of clouds; the song of the ruthless was stilled… And he will destroy on this mountain the shroud that is cast over all peoples, the sheet that is spread over all nations; he will swallow up death forever. Then the Lord will wipe away the tears from all faces, and the disgrace of his people he will take away from all the earth, for the Lord has spoken. It will be said on that day, Lo, this is our God; we have waited for him, so that he might save us. This is the Lord for whom we have waited; let us be glad and rejoice in his salvation.

'Wait for the Lord' is one of the commonest commands in the Old Testament. Individuals were to 'wait' for him, and Israel was to 'wait' for him. Here, the anxious and needy—those terrified by 'the ruthless', by the storms of life and the very thought of death—will one day discover that their deliverance comes from 'the Lord for whom we have waited' (v. 9).

On the whole, though, we do not like waiting, whether it is for a bus or a longed-for event. The whole emphasis today is on pleasure *now*. In God's economy, however, the waiting is essential. During it we learn profound lessons of faith. He is our 'refuge', our 'shelter', our 'shade from the heat' (v. 4). He is the one who silences the terrifying voices. He is also the answer to our innate fear of death as he will 'swallow up death for ever' (v. 8), wiping away the tears of the mourners.

This, says the psalmist, is the work of the God for whom we have 'waited'—not passively, like people at a bus stop, but actively, in prayer, faith and longing.

Waiting for God is not a waste of time, but the best possible way to spend it.

DAVID WINTER

The sound of silence

He said, 'Go out and stand on the mountain before the Lord, for the Lord is about to pass by.' Now there was a great wind, so strong that it was splitting mountains and breaking rocks in pieces before the Lord, but the Lord was not in the wind; and after the wind an earthquake, but the Lord was not in the earthquake; and after the earthquake a fire, but the Lord was not in the fire; and after the fire a sound of sheer silence. When Elijah heard it, he wrapped his face in his mantle and went out and stood at the entrance of the cave. Then there came a voice to him that said, 'What are you doing here, Elijah?'

The 'He' at the beginning of this passage is 'the word of the Lord' (v. 9), so it is by divine guidance that Elijah, feeling abandoned by God, stands on the mountain to be the spectator of a series of dramatic events. First there is a gale, tearing rocks to pieces. That is followed by an earthquake; then there is a fire. Elijah, having been told that the Lord is 'about to pass by' (v. 11), can detect no message in them, no word of comfort or guidance.

Then it happens. In older translations it says that God spoke in 'a still small voice', but the NRSV translates the Hebrew very literally, saying that he actually spoke in the 'sound of sheer silence'—a paradox if ever there was one!

As the noise of the wind, storm and earthquake disappeared, so, in the utter silence of that lonely mountainside, Elijah heard what God wanted to say to him. He did not hear God's words with his ears, but with his spirit. They were not, as it happens, words of comfort, but very specific and solemn guidance. His earthly life was to end, but, before it did, he was to fulfil a vital role in God's purposes.

Here is a man in desperate need who found that, alone in the silence, he could 'hear' what he had not heard as he prayed on his journey to Horeb. Perhaps sometimes even our own words of intercession can drown out the silent voice of God.

DAVID WINTER

Be still and know

There is a river whose streams make glad the city of God, the holy habitation of the Most High. God is in the midst of the city; it shall not be moved; God will help it when the morning dawns. The nations are in an uproar, the kingdoms totter; he utters his voice, the earth melts. The Lord of hosts is with us; the God of Jacob is our refuge. Come, behold the works of the Lord; see what desolations he has brought on the earth. He makes wars cease to the end of the earth; he breaks the bow, and shatters the spear; he burns the shields with fire. 'Be still, and know that I am God! I am exalted among the nations, I am exalted in the earth.'

This is a wonderful psalm, full of poetic visions of the future and a call to the present hearer to take heart from its promises. God dwells in the holy city—Christians will think of the vision of the new Jerusalem in Revelation 21 and 22—but he is active now in the 'tottering' kingdoms of the world as well. 'When the morning dawns' (v. 5), he will make 'wars cease to the end of the earth' (v. 9). Though in our present-day world the 'nations are in uproar', God is still 'with us' ('Emmanuel') and remains our refuge from the storms of life.

We are told to 'behold the works of the Lord' (v. 8), to see his power and majesty. The nations that seem so powerful and the armies which spread such fear are still subject to his rule. Then, in verse 10, comes the key invitation: 'Be still'. While we are 'fretting' and fearful, while we are overwhelmed by the pressures and distractions of the world around us, we may lose sight of the greatest revelation of all: to 'know that I am God' (v. 10). Like Elijah in yesterday's passage, we may need to wait for the silence in order to discover that great truth: 'Be still, and know' (v. 10).

'For thus said the Lord God, the Holy One of Israel: In returning and rest you shall be saved; in quietness and in trust shall be your strength' (Isaiah 30:15).

DAVID WINTER

Creating quietness

Then justice will dwell in the wilderness, and righteousness abide in the fruitful field. The effect of righteousness will be peace, and the result of righteousness, quietness and trust for ever. My people will abide in a peaceful habitation, in secure dwellings, and in quiet resting-places. The forest will disappear completely, and the city will be utterly laid low. Happy will you be who sow beside every stream, who let the ox and the donkey range freely.

How can we find a place of peace in a continually noisy world? We may think ours is the most hectic generation ever to exist (and we may be right), but clearly the psalmist also knew the longing we feel for a 'peaceful habitation' and a 'quiet resting place'.

Of course, as Christians, we are called to live in the mainstream of daily life, bearing our witness and living out our faith in all the hurly-burly, whether it is a crowded supermarket, busy office, noisy classroom or the shouts of the children or grandchildren we are supposed to be looking after. The busier the life, however, the more we need the quiet resting place—some time when we can 'wait on the Lord' in peace.

For the psalmist, there are some interesting pointers here as to how this quiet place can be found: 'The effect of righteousness will be peace, and the result of righteousness, quietness and trust for ever' (v. 17). So, 'righteousness' is the answer, but what does this word mean? The only way most people use it today is as a negative—'self-righteous'. In fact, in the Bible, righteousness simply means 'doing what God requires', seeking to live our lives according to his will for us. Trusting the 'God of peace' is the way to find the peace of God (Philippians 4:7, 9) and to be at peace with our Creator is a sure way to be at peace with his creation!

Pursuing a simple, good life—sowing by every stream and letting the ox and donkey range freely—is the psalmist's own vision of peace. But 'the city will be laid low', too, its noise stilled, as we find the peace of God in our hearts.

DAVID WINTER

Treasuring words

When the angels had left them and gone into heaven, the shepherds said to one another, 'Let us go now to Bethlehem and see this thing that has taken place, which the Lord has made known to us.' So they went with haste and found Mary and Joseph, and the child lying in the manger. When they saw this, they made known what had been told them about this child; and all who heard it were amazed at what the shepherds told them. But Mary treasured all these words and pondered them in her heart. The shepherds returned, glorifying and praising God for all they had heard and seen, as it had been told them.

This is a familiar story—the visit of the shepherds to the stable at Bethlehem. Of course, they had an amazing story to tell, so they lost no time in telling it. What strikes the thoughtful reader, though, is the reaction of the young mother.

Mary—probably still in her teens—had experienced a truly life-changing series of events since the day the angel Gabriel told her that she would be the mother of the long-awaited Messiah. Now it has happened. She is holding in her arms and suckling the one Gabriel called, 'the Son of the Most High' (Luke 1:32). What strength of character, what depth of faith enabled this young woman to remain calm and composed in the light of all that had happened to her?

We are told what the young mother did, while the shepherds went off to tell their astonishing news: she 'treasured all these words' and 'pondered them in her heart' (v. 19). Night-time would come, the stable would be quiet and Mary could treasure in the silence all that had happened and 'ponder' on it. At the end of the excitement of that day, perhaps it was in the treasuring and pondering in the silence of the night that Mary found her own quietness and peace.

To ponder, according to the Oxford English Dictionary, is to 'consider carefully'. The Latin root of the English word means 'weigh' or 'weight', hence the sense of 'weighing something up'. Silence provides an opportunity to weigh things up spiritually—and to make the word of God our treasure.

DAVID WINTER

Making space for silence

That evening, at sunset, they brought to [Jesus] all who were sick or possessed with demons. And the whole city was gathered around the door. And he cured many who were sick with various diseases, and cast out many demons; and he would not permit the demons to speak, because they knew him. In the morning, while it was still very dark, he got up and went out to a deserted place, and there he prayed.

'Pressure of time' is the most common reason we give for failing to make space in our lives for prayer, reflection and 'waiting on God'. We cite our busy lives, the demands of family, home or work. 'There are simply not enough hours in the day,' we say. Well, here is an account of one man's day nearly 2000 years ago. In the course of one Saturday, he went to worship in the synagogue, healed a man with an 'unclean spirit' (v. 26), healed a friend's mother-in-law of a fever, ate a meal she had prepared and, in the evening, found the house besieged by people seeking healing, as 'the whole city was gathered around the door' (v. 33). He healed 'many' (v. 34) who were sick, conducted exorcisms of others and, finally, snatched some sleep.

Surely after such a day this man was entitled to a bit of a lie-in? Far from it: 'while it was still very dark'—long before dawn—'he got up and went out to a deserted place to pray'. However tired he may have felt, he knew that he needed time with his heavenly Father more than an extra (however well-deserved) hour in bed.

The man, of course, is Jesus, the Son of God. If *he* felt such a powerful need to make space for his Father's voice and seek his presence, how much more should we? This is not a plea for worn-out parents and others to abandon their necessary rest, but for all of us to live a more disciplined life, making time (which is a gift from God, after all) our servant, not our master.

Lord, there will be so much to do today. Help me to remember
that the busier I am, the more I need your help.

DAVID WINTER

The secret place of prayer

[Jesus said] 'And whenever you pray, do not be like the hypocrites; for they love to stand and pray in the synagogues and at the street corners, so that they may be seen by others. Truly I tell you, they have received their reward. But whenever you pray, go into your room and shut the door and pray to your Father who is in secret; and your Father who sees in secret will reward you. When you are praying, do not heap up empty phrases as the Gentiles do; for they think that they will be heard because of their many words. Do not be like them, for your Father knows what you need before you ask him.'

It is important to read Jesus' words here in their context. He contrasts the way the 'hypocrites' approach prayer and fasting and the way the 'people of the kingdom' should do it. He is not criticising people who pray in the synagogue (he went there every sabbath), or those who pray with friends and family (as we know the first Christians did: see Acts 12:12). Rather, he is emphasising the essentially inward nature of prayer and such disciplines as fasting, saying that they are to be expressions of an inward impulse, not a public exhibition of piety. Typically, he puts it in vigorous and plain language. When you pray, find a private place (if you can, I suppose) and shut the door. Speak to your 'heavenly Father' (a very intimate title) secretly, and in that way you will be heard.

As for the language of prayer, again, Jesus is blunt. Do not heap up fancy phrases, he says, as the Gentiles tended to do in their prayers to their gods. Do not look for some special 'religious' language. God is not shocked by plain speaking. We need not worry about what words to use, because God reads our hearts: 'Your father knows what you need before you ask' (Matthew 6:8). Also, do not worry if your prayers are short (or long!). It is not the length but the strength that matters.

We should never be deterred from praying because we cannot 'find the right words'. God knows our hearts and it is our inmost longings that he understands and hears.

DAVID WINTER

Shared love

> As God's chosen ones, holy and beloved, clothe yourselves with compassion, kindness, humility, meekness, and patience. Bear with one another and, if anyone has a complaint against another, forgive each other; just as the Lord has forgiven you, so you also must forgive. Above all, clothe yourselves with love, which binds everything together in perfect harmony. And let the peace of Christ rule in your hearts, to which indeed you were called in the one body. And be thankful.

Here are the apostle Paul's secrets for a peaceful and harmonious life. Interestingly, they are set in the context of fellowship: the words 'you' and 'your' are all plural, and the verses we have read are immediately followed by a vivid picture of a group of Christians meeting together for Bible study, prayer and worship (3:16). The silences of prayer are not to be experienced exclusively on our own. There is great blessing in sharing silence, especially in the context of Bible study and worship. The love that Christians can share, born of 'compassion, kindness, humility, meekness, and patience' (v. 12), is at the heart of all that they do together.

This is how the peace of Christ 'rules' in our hearts. The word used by Paul means 'arbitrates': it is the word used for the role of a referee or umpire in the Greek games. It is the presence (or absence) of the peace that creates, or hinders, our sense of closeness to God. The key to this peace is clearly love: 'Above all, clothe yourselves with love' (v. 14), the source of harmony.

Twice in this passage the hearers are urged to 'clothe' (vv. 12, 14) themselves—with compassion and with love. Indeed, wrapping up our lives in the essentials of a peaceful and harmonious life will transform our actions, our words, and our silences.

'Forgive us our sins, as we forgive those who sin against us.' How simple it sounds. What a challenge it often is! Yet, in that very act of forgiving, we may well find the 'peace of God, which surpasses all understanding' (Philippians 4:7).

DAVID WINTER

Suffering and silence

[Jesus] came out and went, as was his custom, to the Mount of Olives; and the disciples followed him. When he reached the place, he said to them, 'Pray that you may not come into the time of trial.' Then he withdrew from them about a stone's throw, knelt down, and prayed, 'Father, if you are willing, remove this cup from me; yet, not my will but yours be done.' Then an angel from heaven appeared to him and gave him strength.

This passage, for all its brevity, tells us so much about Jesus, about prayer, about anxiety and about unwavering faith.

The fact that its setting is the quiet of a beautiful garden on a still April evening makes it even more memorable, for in the silence of Gethsemane a crucial struggle took place. From the moment when Jesus willingly accepted the will of his Father and the bitter 'cup' of suffering (see Psalm 75:8), the great conflict between light and darkness was settled. From that moment, the cross lay ahead, in all its ugliness and cruelty, beyond it lay another garden—the garden of the resurrection and the defeat of darkness and evil.

This was a prayer uttered in agony of mind. You can feel the tension here, in Jesus' request ('Father, if you are willing, remove this cup from me', v. 42)—and in the later description of his sweat falling 'like great drops of blood' (v. 44). Jesus the man did not want to be crucified. What human being would? Jesus the Son of God, however, knew his calling and, if this was the only way to achieve redemption for the human race, then he was prepared to say 'not my will but yours be done' (v. 42). It was a man, one of us, who went to the cross, but it was also as the divine Son of God, the Saviour of the world.

This passage—presumably conveyed by Jesus to the disciples after the resurrection—makes it clear that prayer can sometimes involve agony, sweat, passion. When the issue is as stark as this, words may be few but their power is great.

In the end, Jesus' prayer and, indeed, all our prayers, must end with the same acknowledgement: 'Your will be done.'

DAVID WINTER

Receive children, receive me

This year, the theme for the Women's World Day of Prayer on Friday 4 March is 'Receive children, receive me'. The sequence of passages we will be exploring over the next 14 days cluster around that theme and, through them, we will be reflecting on a number of the many biblical references to children and childhood in both the Old and New Testaments. Some of them stem directly from the teaching and life experiences of Jesus, while others touch on some of the ways in which children were viewed more generally at different time periods in Israelite society.

It would be a mistake to sentimentalise Jesus' view of children. Life for many children throughout the biblical period was fraught with danger, as Jesus' own perilous early months amply demonstrate (Matthew 2:13–23). In our own day, seemingly endless accounts of child cruelty, sex trafficking and general exploitation continue to contaminate the pages of our newspapers.

So, what did Jesus mean when he urged his followers to become like little children? The answer is multifaceted, as the notes that follow aim to reveal. We begin with the shepherds' visit to the baby in the manger, noting the simple, heartfelt trust that enabled them gladly to receive and act on the angels' message, and we follow this with a consideration of the practice of child oblation by looking at the experience of the child Samuel (1 Samuel 3:1–9). We also look at some called by God who plead their youth as an excuse for not doing God's will (Jeremiah 1:4–8) and God's response to their reactions. As adults, we may try to relive our lives and aspirations through our young people, but certain passages challenge such tendencies. When Jesus heals a blind man (John 9:20–22), the need for the grown-up child to speak for himself is raised—a point stressed again by Paul in 1 Corinthians 13:11.

When Jesus urges his disciples to become like little children so that they may enter the kingdom of heaven, he addresses a subtle range of qualities—trust, wonder, acceptance—that we all begin life with but tend to lose as we grow to adulthood. It is in the recovery of such trust and acceptance that our salvation lies.

BARBARA MOSSE

Do not be afraid

In that region there were shepherds living in the fields, keeping watch over their flock by night. Then an angel of the Lord stood before them, and the glory of the Lord shone around them, and they were terrified. But the angel said to them, 'Do not be afraid; for see—I am bringing you good news of great joy for all the people: to you is born this day in the city of David a Saviour, who is the Messiah, the Lord. This will be a sign for you: you will find a child wrapped in bands of cloth and lying in a manger. And suddenly there was with the angel a multitude of the heavenly host, praising God and saying, 'Glory to God in the highest heaven, and on earth peace among those whom he favours!'... So they went with haste.

When he was about 16 years old, the young man who later became Cuthbert of Lindisfarne was working as a shepherd near the River Tweed. His Christian faith was strong and he found that when it was his turn to watch over the sheep during the night, the silent darkness together with the gentle presence of the animals offered a perfect opportunity for prayer. While he was praying during one such night, Cuthbert saw a vision of angels accompanying a human soul to heaven, surrounded by bright light. The next day, he heard that Aidan, the then bishop of Lindisfarne, had died at the precise time of his vision. The realisation of what he had seen changed his life and he determined to become a monk.

Luke's account describes both Jesus—literally a baby—and the experience of the Bethlehem shepherds, who clearly nurtured a child-like openness in their hearts. These first witnesses to the good news of Christ's birth were initially fearful (v. 9), but they believed what they had been told by the angels without question and acted accordingly: 'Let us now go to Bethlehem and see this thing that has taken place...' (v. 15). Are we as ready to see, believe and act?

Awaken us, O Lord, to the beauties of your creation and open our eyes that we may see the wonders and mysteries of your love.

BARBARA MOSSE

Offered to God

Now the boy Samuel was ministering to the Lord under Eli... Then the Lord called, 'Samuel! Samuel!' and he said, 'Here I am!' and ran to Eli, and said, 'Here I am, for you called me.' But he said, 'I did not call; lie down again.'... The Lord called again, 'Samuel!' Samuel got up and went to Eli, and said, 'Here I am, for you called me.' But he said, 'I did not call, my son; lie down again.'... The Lord called Samuel again, a third time. And he got up and went to Eli, and said, 'Here I am, for you called me.' Then Eli perceived that the Lord was calling the boy. Therefore Eli said to Samuel, 'Go, lie down; and if he calls you, you shall say, "Speak, Lord, for your servant is listening."'

Hildegard of Bingen (1098–1179) was a German Benedictine nun, writer, musician and polymath. Thought to have been the tenth child of her family, she was about eight years old when her parents offered her to the Benedictine religious order as a child oblate. She was placed with Jutta, a young woman in her teens. Together they led a life of prayer and practical service and, after Jutta's death, Hildegard became the leader of her monastic community.

As we see in today's account from Samuel's early life, the practice of child oblation has a long history. Samuel was even younger than Hildegard when he was placed with Eli. The previous chapter indicates that he was handed over as soon as he was weaned. Such a practice seems barbaric to us today, and by the end of the twelfth century it had fallen out of favour.

Yet, traces of the practice linger in our services of baptism and thanksgiving for the gift of a child. However incoherent the parents' faith may be, as they bring their child to such services, there remains a deeply held desire to dedicate, to give thanks. The child Samuel reminds us once again, it is often through the youngest and least regarded that God chooses to make his will known to the rest of us.

Jesus said... 'Have you never read, "Out of the mouths of infants and nursing babies you have prepared praise for yourself?"' (Matthew 21:16)

BARBARA MOSSE

'I am only a boy!'

Now the word of the Lord came to me saying, 'Before I formed you in the womb I knew you, and before you were born I consecrated you; I appointed you a prophet to the nations.' Then I said, 'Ah, Lord God! Truly I do not know how to speak, for I am only a boy.' But the Lord said to me, 'Do not say, "I am only a boy"; for you shall go to all to whom I send you, and you shall speak whatever I command you. Do not be afraid of them, for I am with you to deliver you, says the Lord.'

No pressure, then! Sometimes, unlike Samuel in yesterday's passage, the child summoned by God to serve shows some reluctance. It was not unusual for a person to claim youth and/or inexperience as a reason for resisting God's call. Even Moses, who was clearly not a child when God called to him from out of the burning bush (Exodus 3:4), pleads, 'O my Lord, please send someone else' (Exodus 4:13)!

God's reaction to Moses' reluctance is anger, plus the provision of Aaron as spokesman to the people to make up for Moses' inadequacy (Exodus 4:14–16). Jeremiah's plea of 'I am only a boy', however, is met with promise and reassurance (Jeremiah 1:8).

The people whom God calls encompass the vast range of humanity, and their selection often defies our human criteria of assessment. Some are young, like Jeremiah and Samuel; some are old, like Simeon and Anna (Luke 2:22–38); some are of dubious moral character, as was Jacob (Genesis 27); and, occasionally, like Judas, they may apparently fail in their task (Matthew 27:3–5). Sometimes the circumstances of the call involve enormous risk. Mary, just a young girl, could have been stoned for falling pregnant out of wedlock, and the baby Jesus narrowly escaped Herod's massacre, only to become a refugee in a foreign land.

This is challenging stuff. If this seemingly random cross-section of fallible humanity across time has been called to serve the purposes of God's kingdom, then so have you and I.

'Where can I go from your Spirit? Or where can I flee from your presence?'
(Psalm 139:7).

BARBARA MOSSE

'This child is destined... '

Simeon blessed them and said to his mother Mary, 'This child is destined for the falling and the rising of many in Israel, and to be a sign that will be opposed so that the inner thoughts of many will be revealed—and a sword will pierce your own soul too.'

'Jessica-Jane Jones was born on 28 February 2014 at Westland Hospital, Walchester, to Samantha (26) and Jeremy (30) Jones. J-J, as she has already been nicknamed, arrived on time, much to her teacher-mother's approval. Jeremy—an Olympic swimmer—hopes that J-J will follow him into the pool, while artist Samantha hopes her daughter will inherit her creative abilities.'

Here we have a joyful birth announcement, typical of many that appear in our newspapers. Generally they raise a smile as we read of the parents' happy aspirations for their new baby. These hopes may be light-hearted, but, for some, they can have a worrying undercurrent. Some years ago, as chaplain at the Royal College of Music in London, I spent a painful hour with a very distressed 17-year-old. Suzanne, a cellist, had been a member of the college's junior school from the age of ten and was about to audition for the senior college. 'I just don't know what to do,' she sobbed. 'Mum's set on me becoming a professional musician. It'll break her heart if I tell her I don't want to play any more.'

The temptation to live our own unfulfilled ambitions through our young—children, nephews and nieces, godchildren or pupils—can be strong. What were Mary and Joseph's hopes, I wonder, as they brought their baby son to the temple? Simeon's blessing was accompanied by a blunt prophetic warning: 'This child is destined...' (v. 34). It was a reminder to Mary and Joseph and to us too, perhaps, that, although it is natural for our children to be the focus of our love and concern, they nevertheless have lives and futures that are uniquely their own.

Think of any young people you are close to. Do you approve or disapprove of the way they are choosing to live their lives? Are you able to trust them and their futures to God, allowing them the freedom to find their own paths?

BARBARA MOSSE

Why were you searching for me?

Now every year [Jesus'] parents went to Jerusalem for the festival of the Passover. And when he was twelve years old, they went up as usual for the festival. When the festival was ended and they started to return, the boy Jesus stayed behind in Jerusalem, but his parents did not know it... After three days they found him in the temple, sitting among the teachers... When his parents saw him they were astonished; and his mother said to him, 'Child, why have you treated us like this?...' He said to them, 'Why were you searching for me? Did you not know that I must be in my Father's house?' But they did not understand what he said to them.

Christ Discovered in the Temple is a painting by the 14th-century Sienese artist Simone Martini. Mary sits to the left of the picture, her right hand raised in protest towards her son, her face a study in stern incomprehension. Jesus stands opposite, arms folded, staring at his mother with a mutinous face—a picture of rebellious adolescence. Between them, Joseph glares down at Jesus, his left hand on Jesus' shoulder and his right extended towards Mary. It is, as the nun and art historian Sister Wendy Beckett has described, 'an extraordinary evocation of the generation gap' (*The Story of Painting*, Dorling Kindersley, 2000, p. 75).

This is a picture that will resonate with parents and teachers across the world and through time. When we read of this incident in the Gospel, the temptation is to overspiritualise it. Jesus was both God and man, so we do this mystery an injustice if we assume that, in Jesus' case, the normal rules of human growth and development did not apply. Martini's painting manages to capture something unavoidable in the developing parent–child relationship—a precious, though difficult, experience from which both parties can learn.

'Children, obey your parents in the Lord, for this is right. "Honour your father and mother"—this is the first commandment with a promise: "so that it may be well with you and you may live long on the earth." And, fathers, do not provoke your children to anger, but bring them up in the discipline and instruction of the Lord' (Ephesians 6:1–4).

BARBARA MOSSE

What were you arguing about?

Then they came to Capernaum; and when [Jesus] was in the house he asked [his disciples], 'What were you arguing about on the way?' But they were silent, for on the way they had argued with one another about who was the greatest. He sat down, called the twelve, and said to them, 'Whoever wants to be first must be last of all and servant of all.' Then he took a little child and put it among them; and taking it in his arms, he said to them, 'Whoever welcomes one such child in my name welcomes me, and whoever welcomes me welcomes not me but the one who sent me.'

'What were you arguing about?' The discomfort of the disciples in response to Jesus' question is tangible here. We can imagine their embarrassment—the awkward silence, shuffling of feet, the determination not to be the first one to catch Jesus' eye.

We are not told who it was or if any of them had the courage to own up, but Jesus seems to have known anyway. Hot on the heels of Jesus' prediction of his own suffering and death, the disciples' argument about which of them was the greatest seems inappropriate and depressingly banal, yet, at the same time, reassuringly human. How many of us, I wonder, have never compared ourselves with other people, with the resulting feelings of pride and self-satisfaction on the one hand or discouragement on the other?

Jesus' use of a child to illustrate his challenge to the disciples would have stopped them in their tracks. In Israelite society, children (especially boys) were valued, but they were valued as safeguarders of the family's ancestral inheritance rather than as young people with voices and opinions of their own. When Jesus focuses on the importance of the child for a true understanding of his mission, it is not just the disciples' pride that is challenged but their entire worldview.

'For by the grace given to me I say to everyone among you not to think
of yourself more highly than you ought to think, but to think with sober
judgement, each according to the measure of faith that God has assigned'
(Romans 12:3).

BARBARA MOSSE

Out of the mouths...

The blind and the lame came to [Jesus] in the temple, and he cured them. But when the chief priests and the scribes saw the amazing things that he did, and heard the children crying out in the temple, 'Hosanna to the Son of David', they became angry and said to him, 'Do you hear what these are saying?' Jesus said to them, 'Yes; have you never read, "Out of the mouths of infants and nursing babies you have prepared praise for yourself"?' He left them, went out of the city to Bethany, and spent the night there.

Young children, before they learn duplicity and subterfuge from their elders, can be refreshingly and sometimes alarmingly direct. More than one parent has cringed at their child's question, 'Mummy/Daddy, why is that lady so fat?' This usually issued in piercing tones impossible not to overhear. Small children say it the way it is. There is no cruelty intended, it is just that they have not learned to censor their thoughts.

The Pharisees and scribes in the temple expected children to be seen and not heard, to respect the superior knowledge of their elders and betters. The leaders had been driven to distraction by the increasing popularity of Jesus, and the children's joyful cry of praise to the 'Son of David' was the last straw. What could *they* possibly know? They were mere children.

It may be that the children were simply copying what the crowds had cried out when Jesus entered Jerusalem earlier in the day (Matthew 21:9). Whatever the case, whether consciously or unconsciously, they were verbalising a profound and unwelcome truth that the leaders did not wish to acknowledge. The scribes and Pharisees rounded on Jesus, demanding that he share their outrage. Jesus' reply, affirming that God actively intends that his praise and his wisdom be expressed through children, will have done nothing to quell their anger.

What place do children and young people hold within your church?
Are they listened to? Are the older and more experienced members of
the church family open to the possibility that God may speak to them
through the words and actions of the children in their midst?

BARBARA MOSSE

When I was a child

When I was a child, I spoke like a child, I thought like a child, I reasoned like a child; when I became an adult, I put an end to childish ways. For now we see in a mirror, dimly, but then we will see face to face. Now I know only in part; then I will know fully, even as I have been fully known.

The messages we get from scripture about children and childhood can seem somewhat contradictory at times. On the one hand, we have Jesus' firm teaching that unless a person is able to change and become like a child, he or she will never enter the kingdom of heaven (Matthew 18:3), yet here we have Paul telling the Corinthian church that when we become adults, childish ways no longer have any place in our way of dealing with the world (1 Corinthians 13:11). Are these two pieces of teaching contradictory—or only apparently so?

It may be that Jesus' instructions to the Twelve before sending them on their mission are of some help here: 'See, I am sending you out like sheep into the midst of wolves; so be wise as serpents and innocent as doves' (Matthew 10:16). The wisdom that Jesus was urging on them involved an awareness of the dangers they would meet and the need for discernment in their dealings with the people they encountered. This warning to be constantly on their guard could so easily have caused them to degenerate into a fearful, defensive cynicism, however, so, to counter that tendency, the disciples were also urged to be 'innocent as doves'. By this Jesus did not mean for them to act with an unthinking naivety, but instead to remain trustingly open to the essential goodness in people and the wider world.

In order to function effectively in our tasks and relationships, we, like the disciples, need to work at developing this balance between wisdom and innocence. Paul's putting an end to 'childish ways' does not destroy this balance, but simply refers to those aspects of childhood that need to be left behind if we are to grow to full maturity.

In your work and relationships, how easy do you find it to maintain a balance between 'wisdom' and 'innocence'?

BARBARA MOSSE

'He will speak for himself'

The Jews did not believe that he had been blind and had received his sight until they called the parents of the man who had received his sight and asked them, 'Is this your son, who you say was born blind? How then does he now see?' His parents answered, 'We know that this is our son, and that he was born blind; but we do not know how it is that now he sees, nor do we know who opened his eyes. Ask him; he is of age. He will speak for himself.' His parents said this because they were afraid of the Jews; for the Jews had already agreed that anyone who confessed Jesus to be the Messiah would be put out of the synagogue.

The 'child' in today's reading is, in fact, a grown man, although the way in which he is presented to us is, partly, as the child of his parents. This man was born blind and Jesus' healing of his blindness on the sabbath added fuel to the fire of the Pharisees' anger regarding Jesus and his activities. The aftermath of the healing crackles with fear and distrust and, in today's passage, the Pharisees round on the man's parents.

The parents' fear of the Jewish leaders and for their own standing in the synagogue is made blatantly clear: here, they come perilously close to disowning their own son. We may inwardly criticise such a craven and apparently unfeeling attitude, but the sense of menace in their interrogation by the religious authorities is very powerful. So, despite their lack of support for their son, they are making an important spiritual point: 'He is of age. He will speak for himself' (John 9:21). The phrase,God has no grandchildren' may be a bit of an old chestnut, but it contains a profound truth. Our parents' beliefs can only carry us so far. There does come a time in life when we need to think and speak for ourselves.

'We must no longer be children, tossed to and fro and blown about by every wind of doctrine… But speaking the truth in love, we must grow up in every way into him who is the head, into Christ' (Ephesians 4:14–15).

BARBARA MOSSE

A little child shall lead them

The wolf shall live with the lamb, the leopard shall lie down with the kid, the calf and the lion and the fatling together, and a little child shall lead them... The nursing child shall play over the hole of the asp, and the weaned child shall put its hand on the adder's den. They will not hurt or destroy on all my holy mountain; for the earth will be full of the knowledge of the Lord as the waters cover the sea.

We can almost imagine this passage being prefaced by Jesus with, 'The kingdom is like…' —the words he used to introduce his parables of the kingdom in Matthew 13. In Genesis 3, the kingdom is torn apart because of human disobedience, and God rebukes the serpent, the tempter: 'I will put enmity between you and the woman, and between your offspring and hers' (Genesis 3:15).

Today's passage comes from later on in the Old Testament period, when the prophet Isaiah envisages a situation in which the calamity will be reversed. He looks forward to the restoration of God's kingdom, when ancient enmities will be healed and 'the earth will be full of the knowledge of the Lord' (Isaiah 11:9). Central to this vision of a healed and restored creation is an image of children: one leading the reconciled creatures, and the very young who are able to play safely alongside the nests of snakes.

A recurring feature in the lives of St Francis and Celtic saints such as Cuthbert and Columba is that wild creatures seemed able to approach them without fear. Something of the spiritual innocence, inner harmony and integrity of these saints' lives dissolved the fear barrier. So, when Jesus says that we must become 'like children' (Matthew 18:3) to enter the kingdom of heaven, perhaps the child's original innocence is the key to his meaning. Jesus thus challenges us to a simpler way of life and being—one in which we rest in God, having simple trust and openness rather than allowing fear to close us in on ourselves and rule our lives.

How often do we unwittingly create barriers between ourselves and others, due to our own inner tensions?

BARBARA MOSSE

I am the Lord your God

I am the Lord your God... you shall have no other gods before me. You shall not make for yourself an idol, whether in the form of anything that is in the heaven above, or that is on the earth beneath, or that is in the water under the earth. You shall not bow down to them or worship them; for I the Lord your God am a jealous God, punishing children for the iniquity of parents, to the third and fourth generation of those who reject me, but showing steadfast love to the thousandth generation of those who love me and keep my commandments.

Today's passage comes from the beginning of a sequence describing the giving of the ten commandments. The initial demand, 'You shall have no other gods before me' (v. 7), is elaborated in the verses that follow. There is to be no worship of anything but God and, to further emphasise this point, a curse/blessing opposition details the inevitable consequences that the Israelites' choices will have (vv. 8–10).

The promise of God's punishment being visited on the children of the transgressors to the third and fourth generation should bring us up short. Does God really punish children for the sins of their parents? How unjust is that? Today's passage (see also Exodus 20:5; 34:7) indicates clearly that this strand of belief was present in the general religious outlook of the time; even the disciples needed Jesus to correct their thinking on the topic (John 9:2–3).

Perhaps it is helpful to widen our perception of how such a 'curse' could be transmitted. Contemporary evidence suggests that a significant percentage of child abusers were themselves abused as children. To take another example, if a child lives in a home contaminated by its parents' cigarette smoke, the possibility of that child's developing cancer in later life is significantly increased. This outcome will not be consciously 'willed' or intended by the parents, even less by God, but the actions and decisions we make now may well have consequences for our children, for good or for ill.

Can you identify any choices you have made in your own life that could have a negative impact on others?

BARBARA MOSSE

Keep yourselves from idols

We know that those who are born of God do not sin, but the one who was born of God protects them, and the evil one does not touch them. We know that we are God's children, and that the whole world lies under the power of the evil one. And we know that the Son of God has come and has given us understanding so that we may know him who is true; and we are in him who is true, in his Son Jesus Christ. He is the true God and eternal life. Little children, keep yourselves from idols.

John's statement that 'those who are born of God do not sin' (v. 18) seems preposterous to us. We continue to be human, so how can we not sin?

To begin to understand what John means, we may need to adjust the lens of our usual interpretive framework. He is not speaking in the terms we usually adopt—those of church membership or Christian belief and practice. Rather, he is thinking of Christian believers as being born of God and dwelling in Christ. As the author of Colossians put it (3:3), 'Your life is hidden with Christ in God.' Of course, as humans, we will continue to sin; we cannot help it. Despite this, however, as children of our heavenly Father, abiding in Christ, we are held by a divine, indestructible reality.

We are not only children, in John's thinking; we are little children. How do we feel about that? We so often pride ourselves on our ability to manage our own affairs. We desire to be liked and to be seen and appreciated by others for our gifts and abilities. John's terminology hints at a dependency and humility that may not sit comfortably with us. Yet, such acceptance is necessary or we will inevitably fall victim to the idols—illusions—of ambition and self-sufficiency. Hard as it may be for us to accept, there is no true resting place for us outside of that nurturing dynamic of love between Jesus and his Father. It is where we belong.

Can you identify any 'idols' in your own life—or in the life of the church, locally or nationally? How might such idols be challenged?

BARBARA MOSSE

Receive children—receive me

At that time the disciples came to Jesus and asked, 'Who is the greatest in the kingdom of heaven?' He called a child, whom he put among them, and said, 'Truly I tell you, unless you change and become like children, you will never enter the kingdom of heaven... Whoever welcomes one such child in my name welcomes me.'

Earlier in this sequence of readings (Friday 26 February) we reflected on the parallel passage in Mark 9:33–37. We have the same statement from Jesus here ('Truly... unless you change and become like children...'), but Mark's version gave rather more explanation: 'Whoever wants to be first must be last of all and servant of all' (9:35).

Ironically, Matthew's sparser description allows for additional layers of interpretation. In his book, *Everything Belongs: The gift of contemplative prayer*, American Franciscan Richard Rohr writes, 'Jesus uses the image of a child to teach us "beginner's mind". A child is one without ego identity to prove, project, or protect. Little children... respond to what is, not what should be or might be. That's why they cry and squeal with pleasure so much.' As a child begins to grow and move out into the world, a strong sense of self is necessary, but Rohr's thesis is that, carried too far, ego overdevelopment becomes a spiritual deathtrap.

Jesus warned his disciples how hard it is for the rich to enter the kingdom of heaven (Matthew 19:23). We put so much energy into proving ourselves and protecting our identity and possessions that we lose the spontaneity and sense of wonder that we were born with. A good literary example is Scrooge in Charles Dickens' *A Christmas Carol*. This 'squeezing, wrenching, grasping, scraping, clutching, covetous old sinner' was reconnected with his more open-hearted, loving and generous childhood self via the ministrations of the ghosts of Christmas Past, Present and Future. The problem for Scrooge—and for us too, perhaps—was not his wealth and social position as such but the way in which he allowed them to close him off from God and his fellow human beings.

How readily do you identify with Richard Rohr's concept of 'beginner's mind'?

BARBARA MOSSE

Like a weaned child

O Lord, my heart is not lifted up, my eyes are not raised too high; I do not occupy myself with things too great and marvellous for me. But I have calmed and quieted my soul, like a weaned child with its mother; my soul within me is like a weaned child. O Israel, hope in the Lord from this time on and for evermore.

We began this cycle of notes with the shepherds visiting the baby Jesus and his new parents in the stable at Bethlehem. We end with a graphic and powerful image from centuries before—that of a weaned child living quietly with its mother. This picture speaks directly to the psalmist's heart, seeing in the child and its mother a parallel with his own soul, resting trustfully in the heart of God. From New Testament times up to the present day, countless icons and paintings of Mary and Jesus show how this image has continued to resonate in the human soul.

In verse 3, the psalmist draws from his own powerful experience and projects it outwards to embrace the whole nation of Israel. He entreats his people to trust in the Lord with the simplicity and confidence of a small child with its mother. It is in this wider application that we perhaps find our greatest challenge.

Talk of trusting in God tends to roll off our tongues relatively easily, but we may find the reality of living that trust in our daily lives rather more difficult. We like to make our own decisions and to feel we are in control, even when circumstances—such as illness or bereavement—show that the autonomy we seek is an illusion. A tiny child is able to do very little independently and, left to its own resources, will die. These verses invite us to be like that child, relying on God because he is the source of all we need to survive and thrive.

'The Lord is my light and my salvation; whom shall I fear? The Lord is the stronghold of my life; of whom shall I be afraid?... Wait for the Lord; be strong, and let your heart take courage; wait for the Lord!'
(Psalm 27:1, 14)

BARBARA MOSSE

MAY–AUGUST 2016

brf

New Daylight

Sustaining your daily journey with the Bible

Don't forget to renew your annual
subscription to *New Daylight*!

If you enjoy the notes, why not also
consider giving a gift subscription
to a friend or member of your family?

You will find subscription order forms on pages 156 and 157.
New Daylight is also available from your local Christian bookshop.

Fasting in the Old Testament

Fasting is a direct challenge to our Western culture, which plays on indulgence and excess. Whether it is food or leisure, we are encouraged to take all we want without ever considering the consequences. Famine, likewise, is an alien concept to countries that have the power to purchase most things they want and can eat strawberries in December whatever the cost. Yet, in a society of strangely contrasting scenes, we have, on the one hand, supermarket shelves groaning with seemingly endless varieties of food and, on the other hand, food banks becoming more and more necessary for some people to survive.

There are all kinds of myths surrounding fasting, some of them coming from the Christian church. Some Christians worry that fasting is open to abuse on many fronts: that it is bad for your health, it is legalistic, it leads to excesses of asceticism, it is associated with other religions or it is simply weird. Fasting, however, also has strong advocates in certain parts of the church: it is good for the health, it leads to increased powers of concentration and increased effectiveness in intercessory prayer, it aids guidance in decision making, and it leads to deliverance from bondage of various kinds.

Fast days and fast seasons, including Lent and Advent, continue to play a part in the liturgical and spiritual observances of some Christians. Fish on Fridays and abstinence from wine or chocolate in Lent help people to think about what binds them—not only in terms of food but also habits and things we take for granted. They remind us that many people go without as a matter of course.

Jesus seems to have taken fasting for granted, for he said, '*Whenever* you fast', not '*If* you fast', to his disciples (Matthew 6:16, NIV). There is a surprisingly large number of references to fasting as well as famine in the Old Testament. Fasting may be voluntary (though not always), but famine is generally beyond human control. As we shall see, though, both may go beyond a physical lack of food. As with many physical conditions, fasting and famine have important things to teach us about God and how we are to live in the light of his word to us.

ELIZABETH HOARE

Fasting and the Day of Atonement

'This is to be a lasting ordinance for you: on the tenth day of the seventh month you must deny yourselves and not do any work—whether native-born or a foreigner residing among you—because on this day atonement will be made for you, to cleanse you. Then, before the Lord, you will be clean from all your sins. It is a day of sabbath rest, and you must deny yourselves; it is a lasting ordinance.'

On this day only, Aaron entered into the holiest part of the temple to offer sacrifices to God to atone for his own sins and those of the people. Chapter 16 describes in meticulous detail the procedure he was to undergo, but these verses indicate that everyone was to observe this outward practice of an inward repentance.

Verse 29 is translated as 'deny yourselves' (NIV and NRSV) or 'afflict yourselves' (RSV) and also means 'fast' or 'abstain from'. Fasting was a way of showing sorrow for sin as it provided a means of chastening yourself and showing humility in the face of God's holiness. Some things are too important for anything else to distract from them, even the ordinary necessities of life.

People of the Jewish faith continue to observe the Day of Atonement, also known as Yom Kippur, with prayer and fasting, but the principle of atonement for sin has immense significance for Christians, too. The sprinkling of blood (see Leviticus 16:14–15) takes us straight to the cross and the death of Jesus, who made atonement there for the sins of the whole world (Romans 5:6–11). The fasting associated with the Day of Atonement was primarily about sorrow for sin.

While Christians believe that the righteousness we receive from God is all his doing and nothing we do can add anything to it, fasting may still be an appropriate response to sorrow for sin. It may help us reflect on the things that bind us, which we need to let go. The small sacrifice of giving up a few meals may also help us remember the great sacrifice made for us on the cross by the Lord Jesus.

'If any want to become my followers, let them deny themselves and take up their cross daily and follow me' (Luke 9:23, NRSV).

ELIZABETH HOARE

True and false fasting

Is not this the kind of fasting I have chosen: to loose the chains of injustice and untie the cords of the yoke, to set the oppressed free and break every yoke? Is it not to share your food with the hungry and to provide the poor wanderer with shelter—when you see the naked, to clothe them, and not to turn away from your own flesh and blood? Then your light will break forth like the dawn, and your healing will quickly appear; then your righteousness will go before you, and the glory of the Lord will be your rear guard. Then you will call, and the Lord will answer; you will cry for help, and he will say: here am I.

One of the temptations of outward religious acts is to perform them ostentatiously in order to impress. The scribes in Jesus' day fell into this temptation and, thus, received his condemnation. Grandiose outward gestures are worse than useless if they conceal hearts that are hard and unreceptive to God's call. 'Why have we fasted… and you have not seen it?' the people of Isaiah's day cried (see 58:3). It was because of the disconnection between the outward gesture and the inward attitude.

The outcome of true fasting is concerned with issues of justice and acts of mercy. It must be accompanied by a setting free of the oppressed, sharing with those who have nothing and providing shelter for those with nowhere to go. It must involve clothing the naked and engaging with the world rather than withdrawing from it (v. 7). Fasting, then, is here redefined as social reform (v. 6), loving care (v. 7) and a forgoing of the desire to accuse ('Do away with… the pointing finger and malicious talk', v. 9b). As such, it points to the way in which Jesus interpreted the law and helps us to put fasting in its proper place.

All of this reshaping comes with a promise in response to the lament of Isaiah 58:3: 'Then you will call, and the Lord will answer; you will cry for help, and he will say: here am I' (v. 9; compare James 4:3, 8–10).

Have you ever been tempted to put on a show of piety
to conceal a hard heart?

ELIZABETH HOARE

Fasting and fitness: Daniel

Daniel then said to the guard whom the chief official had appointed over Daniel, Hananiah, Mishael and Azariah, 'Please test your servants for ten days: give us nothing but vegetables to eat and water to drink. Then compare our appearance with that of the young men who eat the royal food, and treat your servants in accordance with what you see.' So he agreed to this and tested them for ten days. At the end of the ten days they looked healthier and better nourished than any of the young men who ate the royal food. So the guard took away their choice food and the wine they were to drink and gave them vegetables instead. To these four young men God gave knowledge and understanding of all kinds of literature and learning. And Daniel could understand visions and dreams of all kinds.

One of the benefits that advocates of fasting identify is that it leads to better health all round. Fasting tends to make us think more carefully about not only what we have given up but also what we put into our bodies in general. People who fast are more likely to eat healthily at other times. There may even be a spiritual dimension to this, in that if our bodies *are* the temple of the Holy Spirit, as Paul teaches (1 Corinthians 6:19), we should take proper care of them in terms of what we eat.

Daniel and his friends had been forcibly removed from their homeland and were living in exile at the court of a foreign despot. In what was an extremely risky strategy, Daniel refused to eat the royal rations. Of course, the story is not recorded in order to promote a vegetarian and teetotal diet. It is about keeping oneself pure and undefiled by the lure of things that could lead to compromise. Daniel and his friends could so easily have forgotten home and their God and thrown themselves into survival and, indeed, advancement in the court of Nebuchadnezzar. The vegetables and water symbolised their commitment to giving single-hearted service to the living God.

Is there anything in your life at present that you would be better off without?

ELIZABETH HOARE

Fasting and mourning: David

David pleaded with God for the child. He fasted and spent the nights lying in sackcloth on the ground. The elders of his household stood beside him to get him up from the ground, but he refused, and he would not eat any food with them. On the seventh day the child died... David noticed that his servants were whispering among themselves, and he realised that the child was dead. 'Is the child dead?' he asked. 'Yes,' they replied, 'he is dead.' Then David got up from the ground. After he had washed, put on lotions and changed his clothes, he went into the house of the Lord and worshipped. Then he went to his own house, and at his request they served him food, and he ate.

Did David think that if he showed more outward sorrow for his sin in stealing Uriah's wife and then murdering him, the child's life might be saved? Here, fasting is seen as an aspect of repentance—the outward sign of inward contrition. In this context, it is closely associated with earnest prayer. David pleaded with God for the child's life and refused to be comforted or persuaded to moderate his behaviour until he received an answer (vv. 16–17). It seems that while the child lived, there was still hope in David's mind that God might spare him.

David may have been distraught with grief, but there may have been other things going on also. David was treating his body with the contempt with which he had treated the life of Uriah the Hittite, but, once the child died, David got up, cleaned himself up, worshipped and then ate. While there was uncertainty, David fasted and prayed. When the matter was closed, he accepted it in a sober but realistic manner. Fasting was part of David's sorrowful repentance and pleading in the in-between time—that is, between the pronouncement of the judgement and its subsequent outworking. The fasting humbled David and kept him focused in his prayer. Though he could not undo what had been done, he was able to accept the situation and eventually go forward to experience God's blessing again (vv. 24–25).

'A broken and contrite heart, O God, you will not despise' (Psalm 51:17).

ELIZABETH HOARE

Fasting and mourning: Hannah

Whenever Hannah went up to the house of the Lord, her rival provoked her till she wept and would not eat. Her husband Elkanah would say to her, 'Hannah, why are you weeping? Why don't you eat? Why are you downhearted? Don't I mean more to you than ten sons?'... In her deep anguish Hannah prayed to the Lord, weeping bitterly. And she made a vow, saying, 'Lord Almighty, if you will only look upon your servant's misery and remember me, and not forget your servant but give her a son, then I will give him to the Lord for all the days of his life, and no razor will ever be used on his head.'

Grief can make us unable to eat. Our bodies seem to shut down and the very sight of food turns our stomachs. We neglect ourselves and self-care drops to the bottom of our thoughts. One of the most useful things we can do for a grieving person is to make them a hot drink and encourage them to eat simple food to sustain them, if they can face it.

Hannah's childlessness rendered her inconsolable. Not only did she have to bear her private grief in the face of Elkanah's children from his other wife, Peninnah, but also she had to endure the latter's ongoing taunts. In addition, she had to cope with the public disgrace that childlessness carried with it in her culture at that time. Children were a sign of God's favour and blessing. There is little wonder that food lost all its appeal for this barren and griefstricken woman.

It is interesting that Elkanah sought to demonstrate his love with food, by giving Hannah a double portion of the sacrifices made at Shiloh (v. 5), but Hannah would have none of it. Her grief went on for years until God heard her plea and at last Hannah bore her first child, whom she dedicated to the Lord. Interestingly, he was to be a Nazirite, so would never drink any alcoholic beverages, demonstrating his dedication to God by abstaining from them.

Pray for those who remain childless despite years of longing and waiting in faith.

ELIZABETH HOARE

Fasting and deceit: Ahab and Naboth

So Ahab went home, sullen and angry because Naboth the Jezreelite had said, 'I will not give you the inheritance of my ancestors.' He lay on his bed sulking and refused to eat. His wife Jezebel came in and asked him, 'Why are you so sullen? Why won't you eat?' He answered her, 'Because I said to Naboth the Jezreelite, "Sell me your vineyard; or if you prefer, I will give you another vineyard in its place." But he said, "I will not give you my vineyard."' Jezebel his wife said, 'Is this how you act as king over Israel? Get up and eat! Cheer up. I'll get you the vineyard of Naboth the Jezreelite.' So she wrote letters in Ahab's name, placed his seal on them, and sent them to the elders and nobles who lived in Naboth's city with him. In those letters she wrote: 'Proclaim a day of fasting and give Naboth a prominent seat among the people.'

Here are two examples of fasting for the wrong purposes, set in a story about a vineyard, a symbol of blessing and abundance (1 Kings 4:25).

Ahab fell into a sulk and refused food because Naboth would not give up his vineyard (v. 4). Ahab's wife, who was used to getting her own way, persuaded Ahab to eat while she ordered a public fast and a solemn assembly to be proclaimed (21: 9). The purpose of this subterfuge was to trap Naboth and ensure his destruction. Fasting is used in this story as a way of practising deceit and betraying an innocent human being. It is therefore a complete perversion of something designed to show integrity.

The story does not end there, however. When confronted by Elijah, Ahab tore his clothes, put on sackcloth and fasted—this time in repentance. God responded with mercy. Did Ahab deserve it? Not at all, but God's mercy is never deserved and no one is beyond its reach—even someone who had sold himself 'to do evil in the eyes of the Lord' (v. 18).

Merciful Lord, who forgives the sins of all who are penitent,
may we never see ourselves as beyond your mercy, nor assume that
there is no forgiveness for someone else. Amen

ELIZABETH HOARE

Fasting and protection: Ezra

There, by the Ahava Canal, I proclaimed a fast, so that we might humble ourselves before our God and ask him for a safe journey for us and our children, with all our possessions. I was ashamed to ask the king for soldiers and horsemen to protect us from enemies on the road, because we had told the king, 'The gracious hand of our God is on everyone who looks to him, but his great anger is against all who forsake him.' So we fasted and petitioned our God about this, and he answered our prayer.

Ezra was soon to fast in repentance on behalf of his people (9:3–5), but here he proclaimed a fast in order to seek God's protection on the journey home to Jerusalem. He had gathered a band of leading men to accompany him (7:28) and now they had to cross the river, together with their children and chattels.

It seems that Ezra could have settled for the practical solution and asked for soldiers to protect them, but he felt this would be a shameful way to proceed because he had expressed confidence in God. Instead, he turned directly to God. Calling a fast demonstrated the seriousness of the request and also the earnestness of the people seeking God's help.

How often do we say that we trust God, yet, when it comes to the test, we prefer to do things in our own strength? Ezra refused to succumb to this temptation. Abstaining from food was a sign that the people were determined to rely on God alone and not on any other form of help. Fasting is never a magical ploy to manipulate God into doing what we want. It is not a means of asking him to bless our plans. Ezra was returning to Jerusalem in obedience to God and therefore trusted that God would supply the means to get him there.

Fasting has a spiritual purpose to it, as this glimpse into Ezra's story shows. It can be a helpful tool in committing ourselves to pray in a clear-headed and submissive way. Many Christians have testified to receiving the guidance they had sought by combining prayer and fasting.

Pray for all those facing danger today.

ELIZABETH HOARE

Fasting and protection: Jehoshaphat

After this, the Moabites and Ammonites with some of the Meunites came to make war against Jehoshaphat. Some people came and told Jehoshaphat, 'A vast army is coming against you from Edom, from the other side of the Dead Sea. It is already in Hazezon Tamar' (that is, En Gedi). Alarmed, Jehoshaphat resolved to enquire of the Lord, and he proclaimed a fast for all Judah. The people of Judah came together to seek help from the Lord; indeed, they came from every town in Judah to seek him.

In 1756, King George II called a national day of prayer and fasting in Britain in the face of invasion by the French. John Wesley wrote, 'Every church in the city was more than full and a solemn seriousness sat on every face. Surely God heareth prayer, and there will be a lengthening of our tranquillity.'

Like the story of Ezra, Jehoshaphat's call to the people to fast was a public one-off event—and, as with King George, it was because of a national emergency. What was he to do in the face of such a grave situation? In his prayer, he acknowledged that 'we have no power to face this vast army that is attacking us. We do not know what to do, but our eyes are on you' (v. 12).

There were two particularly remarkable results of this period of prayer and fasting, in addition to the victory that God granted them. First, God spoke to the people via his prophets and told them not to be afraid, for the battle belonged to the Lord (v. 15). Second, the people worshipped in praise and song (v. 21). Focusing on God by fasting and praying enabled the people to get things into true perspective.

When we do not know what to do, where do we instinctively turn? It is easy to panic or run to the nearest safety net without thinking whether or not it is what God has provided. In the situation facing Jehoshaphat, a corporate fast kept all the people focused on God and his protection and enabled him to act decisively in obedience and trust.

Could fasting help you if you are facing something that you do not know how to approach?

ELIZABETH HOARE

Famine and God's silence

'In that day,' declares the Sovereign Lord, 'I will make the sun go down at noon and darken the earth in broad daylight. I will turn your religious festivals into mourning and all your singing into weeping. I will make all of you wear sackcloth and shave your heads. I will make that time like mourning for an only son and the end of it like a bitter day. The days are coming,' declares the Sovereign Lord, 'when I will send a famine through the land—not a famine of food or a thirst for water, but a famine of hearing the words of the Lord.'

When Amos prophesied to the northern kingdom, it was outwardly prosperous, but all kinds of evil were rife in the land. Amos was called to pronounce God's coming judgement on people who considered themselves secure and resented any reproof (5:10). Those with power made the measure of wheat small in relation to the shekel, thus robbing the poor of life's necessities. God hates injustice like this and vowed vengeance by sending a famine.

This famine did not consist of crop failure or the absence of rain, however—it was a famine of 'hearing the words of the Lord' (8:11). The picture that follows is of people who are bewildered and rudderless, rushing here and there, looking for God's word but never finding it. Those who caused physical hunger for the weak and needy were now afflicted with hunger themselves, but of a different order.

Much later, Jesus was to look on Jerusalem and weep because, having refused for so long to recognise the things that made for peace, these things became hidden from their eyes. In today's world, too, we witness hunger among the poor and behaviour like that described by Amos— people running to and fro, seeking meaning, pleasure and security in so many wrong places because of a famine caused by failure to heed God's words of life to us. It is a self-inflicted famine, because God has spoken and made his ways known.

What response do you make to those situations where God seems to have imposed a famine of hearing his word?

ELIZABETH HOARE

Famine and the making of a leader

During the seven years of abundance the land produced plentifully. Joseph collected all the food produced in those seven years of abundance in Egypt and stored it in the cities. In each city he put the food grown in the fields surrounding it. Joseph stored up huge quantities of grain, like the sand of the sea; it was so much that he stopped keeping records because it was beyond measure.

Famine has the capacity to reduce people to pale shadows of themselves with no thought beyond the immediate need for sustenance. Famine usually catches people unprepared; it is rare for there to be a warning as there was here, due to Pharaoh's strange dreams of fat and thin cows and ears of corn. It was Joseph's moment and enabled him to be God's person in an alien land.

Once an arrogant youth, Joseph not only supplied the interpretation of Pharaoh's dreams but he also advised wise and careful stewardship of the plentiful harvests, storing up supplies to see them through the coming famine. His shrewd words carried weight and Joseph found himself appointed second in the land, wielding great power. When the long period of hunger came, only Egypt had food; all the other nations starved. Then, 'all the world came to Egypt to buy grain from Joseph, because the famine was severe everywhere' (v. 57).

In Joseph, Christians have found many of the characteristics of Jesus Christ, who is the bread of life. Just as Pharaoh directed those in need to go to Joseph, we are directed to find in Christ all that we need and to point the way to him to others, rather like (as evangelist D.T. Niles put it) 'one beggar telling another where to find bread'.

He is also someone for us to ponder as we think about our own stewardship. Joseph was found to be trustworthy. Huge trust was invested in him on this basis and he remained consistently faithful to repaying that trust.

Are we laying up treasure in heaven? Are we storing up qualities and resources that will sustain us in this world in times of spiritual famine?

ELIZABETH HOARE

Famine and migration: Jacob

Then Joseph said to his brothers, 'Come close to me.' When they had done so, he said, 'I am your brother Joseph, the one you sold into Egypt! And now, do not be distressed and do not be angry with yourselves for selling me here, because it was to save lives that God sent me ahead of you. For two years now there has been famine in the land, and for the next five years there will be no ploughing and reaping. But God sent me ahead of you to preserve for you a remnant on earth and to save your lives by a great deliverance.'

Everyone in Jacob's extended family and all their possessions, young and old, livestock and chattels, had to be moved en masse to the new destination. From this foreign land, God would subsequently rescue his embryonic nation by the hand of Moses and fashion a people for himself.

Once again, we see how famine played its part in bringing about God's purposes. Jacob initially had no intention of moving to Egypt. Instead, he sent his sons, with the exception of Benjamin, to find food and bring it home (43:1–5), for he had heard that there was food there. Little did he know his lost son, Joseph, was responsible for building up the grain reserves that were now feeding the whole region.

Imagine Jacob's reaction when he heard first of all that his beloved Joseph was still alive. Then imagine him setting out, frail and chastened by so many life experiences. Again, God spoke to him and reminded him who it was who had watched over him all his days: 'I am God, the God of your father… Do not be afraid' (46:3). Once again he promised to go with him to keep him safe and provide for him. Thus, he would remain faithful to his original promise to Abraham, to make of him a great nation.

'I am confident of this, that the one who began a good work among you will bring it to completion by the day of Jesus Christ'
(Philippians 1:6, NRSV).

ELIZABETH HOARE

89

Famine and migration: Ruth

In the days when the judges ruled, there was a famine in the land. So a man from Bethlehem in Judah, together with his wife and two sons, went to live for a while in the country of Moab. The man's name was Elimelek, his wife's name was Naomi, and the names of his two sons were Mahlon and Kilion. They were Ephrathites from Bethlehem, Judah. And they went to Moab and lived there. Now Elimelek, Naomi's husband, died, and she was left with her two sons. They married Moabite women, one named Orpah and the other Ruth. After they had lived there about ten years, both Mahlon and Kilion also died, and Naomi was left without her two sons and her husband.

Famine has caused the movement of individuals and whole nations since the dawn of time. The story of Ruth is a sad but beautiful tale of love, loyalty and God's provision in one small family. When Naomi set off for home, Ruth vowed to accompany her wherever it took her. Thus, she found herself in an alien land, as Naomi had done before her. Famine had indirectly caused her life to take a different turn from the one she might have anticipated as she grew up in her own land.

Today we continue to witness the progress of huge migrations of people across the globe, often because of famine. People escaping famine are no longer 'out there' somewhere, but here in our midst.

Ruth's story became intertwined with that of God's promised Messiah, for she is named at the end of the book as an ancestor of King David and so also of Jesus himself (4:18–22). As we read the whole story of Ruth, we see the importance of generosity on the part of Boaz, confidence that God will provide on the part of Naomi and trusting obedience on the part of Ruth herself. Out of these interrelated qualities, God wove the pattern of his purposes for the whole world.

Hebrews urges us to show hospitality to strangers: 'for by so doing some people have shown hospitality to angels without knowing it' (Hebrews 13:2). Pray that we might show generosity to those in need and become part of his purposes for today's world.

ELIZABETH HOARE

Famine, sword and pestilence

After that, declares the Lord, I will give Zedekiah king of Judah, his officials and the people in this city who survive the plague, sword and famine, into the hands of Nebuchadnezzar king of Babylon and to their enemies who want to kill them. He will put them to the sword; he will show them no mercy or pity or compassion. Furthermore, tell the people, 'This is what the Lord says: see, I am setting before you the way of life and the way of death. Whoever stays in this city will die by the sword, famine or plague. But whoever goes out and surrenders to the Babylonians who are besieging you will live; they will escape with their lives.'

Many times in the Bible, famine, sword and pestilence are linked together, especially in the prophecies of Jeremiah and Ezekiel. They come together as God's judgement on a repeatedly disobedient and faithless people. This reading from Jeremiah is a terrible prophecy of the destruction of Jerusalem and the end of the nation as they knew it. Yet, it is those who remain in the city who will suffer. The way to life lies in surrender to the coming punishment, not in clinging to the old order and hoping for rescue that way.

Famine, war and disease continue to stalk the earth and people are at their mercy in many places. How do we deal with the suffering victims of hunger, often due to wars not of their making? There is nothing spiritually edifying in the sight of children begging for bread and none being given to them (Lamentations 4:4). Famine is an enforced fast that wreaks havoc in its wake.

Jesus also linked famine, war and pestilence in his teaching about the impending doom hanging over Jerusalem (for example, in Matthew 24:7). As he spoke of these terrible things, he also preached good news and, in the parable of the sheep and the goats, commended those who fed the hungry and gave drink to the thirsty.

As we draw strength from the gospel truth that not 'famine, or nakedness, or peril, or sword' can separate us from the love of God (Romans 8:35, NRSV), we are also called to feed the hungry and protect the weak.

ELIZABETH HOARE

Fasting and intercession

When I looked, I saw that you had sinned against the Lord your God; you had made for yourselves an idol cast in the shape of a calf. You had turned aside quickly from the way that the Lord had commanded you. So I took the two tablets and threw them out of my hands, breaking them to pieces before your eyes. Then once again I fell prostrate before the Lord for forty days and forty nights; I ate no bread and drank no water, because of all the sin you had committed, doing what was evil in the Lord's sight and so arousing his anger. I feared the anger and wrath of the Lord, for he was angry enough with you to destroy you. But again the Lord listened to me.

Imagine Moses' reaction as he came down from the mountain where he had spent 40 days and nights with the living and holy God, only to be confronted with a golden calf and the people cavorting around and worshipping it. He smashed the two tablets, on which were carved God's good commandments, as a symbolic shattering of the promise they held.

Moses fell down prostrate before God in sorrow, repentance and fear for another 40 days and nights. He was afraid that the Lord would be so angry he would destroy the people; and so, not for the first time, Moses stood in the breach and interceded. His own anger was subsumed in his immediate concern for his people's very existence. Abstaining from food and drink on this occasion demonstrates the seriousness of the situation and of Moses' love and commitment to the people he had led through the desert. It also demonstrates his faith in God's mercy: 'Again the Lord listened to me' (v. 19).

The length of Moses' fast was linked to the giving of the law at a pivotal moment in Israel's history, and it would not be advisable for us to attempt to match it. The length of the fast is not the point. God may lead us to set time aside to intercede on behalf of others in a way that goes beyond the norms of our regular times of prayer. Fasting from food could increase both our intention and our attention.

May your goodness kindle in me, dear Lord, the desire to intercede for the world you love.

ELIZABETH HOARE

Luke's Easter journey

The idea that a journey is much more than a physical event is not unique to Christianity, although the practice of going on a pilgrimage is at least as strong for Christians as it is for anyone else. The Gospels invite us to make a particular kind of journey—not to trace the events as from a distance or with cold detachment, but, rather, to step in and walk alongside, hearing the noises, sensing the mood and letting the smells waft over us. In a sense, this is a journey that passes through us rather than asking us to go anywhere physically.

Luke's Easter journey brings the key events of the life and death of Jesus to the fore. Crowds that gather as he arrives in Jerusalem's hustle and bustle prove a fickle bunch, their mood altering rapidly as the kind of kingship he brings becomes more apparent. We see a change in Jesus as he weeps over the city of peace.

The drama of his agony in the garden of Gethsemane is followed by a betrayal that has the sharpest edge because a colleague and friend devises the plot. This is followed by his crucifixion and death, with two criminals at his side. One of these men has travelled far from the ruination that brought him to this place and Luke records his last words, which usher him into a fullness of life he could not have ever imagined.

The greater part of this series of notes is given to the discovery—first by some women and then other disciples—of a grave which is now empty. From this tantalising place of wonder, they meet the one who had died but is now alive and calling them to new faith and adventure. Our task is to hear that call again and let resurrection faith arrive, then dwell in us. If we do, like the disciples, we will journey out on an adventure that will change everything. That is the challenge for us—to become part of Luke's Easter journey. Are you ready?

ANDY JOHN

The king shows up

As he was now approaching the path down from the Mount of Olives, the whole multitude of the disciples began to praise God joyfully with a loud voice for all the deeds of power that they had seen, saying, 'Blessed is the king who comes in the name of the Lord! Peace in heaven, and glory in the highest heaven!' Some of the Pharisees in the crowd said to him, 'Teacher, order your disciples to stop.' He answered, 'I tell you, if these were silent, the stones would shout out.'

Jesus' entry into Jerusalem could not have been more provocative. This was an outrageous statement to make. The crowds heralded his arrival (v. 38), the hordes spoke of his awesome deeds, the religious authorities were apoplectic and, to cap it all, Jesus seemed to lap it up (v. 40) and invite even further attention and adulation.

At the start of this series of notes on Luke's Easter journey, we find ourselves travelling, too—with the good doctor—into Jerusalem. It is a time of fervour. The backdrop has two elements: the widely held view that the Messiah will soon come to ransom Israel and the impending festival of Passover, when Israel celebrates the people's exodus from Egypt. The Romans are edgy, keen to snuff out anything that might look like rebellion, and the religious authorities are resolute that any claim to their position will be strangled early on.

So, Jesus is welcomed as a king. King Jesus, leader of armies and thousands who will rise up with spears and hooks—or not. There is a clue in his arrival on the colt, the foal of an ass—not the standard mode of transport for kings and princes. Here, too, we see a picture of the kingdom and reign he seeks to bring. It will not be a forced new form of occupation, not a government of benevolent dictation, but a rule of peace and love in which hearts are won, lives transformed and justice delivered. This is where Luke is taking us on this journey and he invites us, at the outset, to ask this simple question: 'What sort of king?'

How does the kingdom of Jesus contrast with the reign of the civil and religious authorities in his time and today?

ANDY JOHN

The city of peace

As he came near and saw the city, he wept over it, saying, 'If you, even you, had only recognised on this day the things that make for peace! But now they are hidden from your eyes. Indeed, the days will come upon you, when your enemies will set up ramparts around you and surround you, and hem you in on every side... because you did not recognise the time of your visitation from God.'

You might ask what the first deed and act of a newly crowned king should be. What are the edicts that need to be signed off and the important people who need to be appeased? How is the economy responding and what is the stock market saying (pigeons down to an all-time low, I hear)?

Jesus' first act was to cry. As he saw the great city, the so-called city of peace, he wept. There are few occasions when Jesus displays emotion of this sort. He cried at the tomb of Lazarus (John 11:35) and later we hear that his anguish was so great in Gethsemane that his sweat fell like drops of blood (Luke 22:44). Here, too, as he stands high above the city of David, his heart is broken. The flow of tears becomes a prayer that even today things might change, the future might be different and they might know what the day of the Lord means.

I have wondered what Jesus sees when he looks at his church. Do you think he weeps still? Somehow, in the eternity of the God who rejoices over us too, and sends the Spirit to reshape and reform, are there still tears shed over our worst sins?

We should take some things from today's part of the journey. First, the compassion of the Lord. His heart can break—over sin and injustice and wickedness—yet his reign of peace and grace is not without strength. That strength holds us accountable. We do know the things that make for peace, even as they cost us in terms of faithful obedience and service.

What does this story tell us about God, the one who can shed tears and feel anguish over a lost and broken world?

ANDY JOHN

The punchline

'Then the owner of the vineyard said, "What shall I do? I will send my beloved son; perhaps they will respect him." But when the tenants saw him, they discussed it among themselves and said, "This is the heir; let us kill him so that the inheritance may be ours." So they threw him out of the vineyard and killed him. What then will the owner of the vineyard do to them? He will come and destroy those tenants and give the vineyard to others.' When they heard this, they said, 'Heaven forbid!'

Although it may not be physically demanding, this journey is not a comfortable one. There are some encounters that are more than challenging. You will probably know that parables, classically understood, are earthly stories with a heavenly meaning. Our passage today includes a parable of this sort, but it has a sting in the tail, too (v. 19).

Jesus is the master storyteller. He weaves the familiar in new and exciting ways so that the heart of the message becomes accessible, yet, tantalisingly, is kept from us. His stories are real and vivid, but also elusive and mysterious. We can almost imagine his listeners saying, 'Oh, not another one about a vineyard…' and 'We've heard it before, tell us a new one!' As Jesus begins to develop the plot, however, they become more intrigued.

Because Jesus challenged the religious authorities, they planned to kill him (v. 19). The scene of conflict, which was soon to find its climax in Jesus' death on the cross, finds an early echo here in the disagreement between a religious body that rejects Jesus' claims and Jesus, who was determined to follow the course set by the Father, seeing it through to the end. We can see where all of this is leading and sense that the message and messenger are of a piece. To bring about the kingdom of God, all powers and peoples must give way. If they will not, they and all the sins of the world will be gathered up on to Calvary's tree in judgement and grace. The shadow of the cross is near.

The kingdom of God brings peace, but what must go if its claims are to be fully accepted and embraced?

ANDY JOHN

The kingdom and generosity

He looked up and saw rich people putting their gifts into the treasury; he also saw a poor widow put in two small copper coins. He said, 'Truly I tell you, this poor widow has put in more than all of them; for all of them have contributed out of their abundance, but she out of her poverty has put in all she had to live on.'

There is no better way to create conflict or put people's noses out of joint than with a good old-fashioned put-down. The one in today's passage is the kind that would send anyone either scuttling for cover or turning to fight, but the subject of this latest little bout is none other than the little old lady from No. 2 Temple Street in the Old Quarter.

The issue at stake in the passage turns on the question of generosity. The contrast is between those who parade themselves and are adorned with riches and someone who is perhaps more modestly attired, but abounds with inner treasures. With it, of course, something is being said about the kingdom and about God. The kingdom is fundamentally about God's astonishing love and grace breaking into our lives. You see it in the lives of people who—so captivated by it, understanding its wealth and beauty—give themselves up to it, somehow allowing it to become a part of them and, in turn, reflecting it in human actions for others to see. Without boast or pomp, our unsung heroine in the passage above does just this: she shows us what the kingdom means and does.

If this riled the religious authorities, we might think about our own response. How far has the tide of the kingdom's waters flowed into my life? Am I challenged by the widow or dismissive? Perhaps I can devise powerful and convincing arguments that shield me from the kind of message such a story excites? We only need look in Jesus' eyes as we recount them.

The kingdom comes in many ways and shows us what God is like. Happy are those who see the treasure and give themselves up for this pearl of great price.

ANDY JOHN

Bread and wine, body and blood

Then [Jesus] took a loaf of bread, and when he had given thanks, he broke it and gave it to them, saying, 'This is my body, which is given for you. Do this in remembrance of me.' And he did the same with the cup after supper, saying, 'This cup that is poured out for you is the new covenant in my blood.'

When Jesus shared the bread and wine with his disciples, he did what the countless faithful had done for centuries. The elements he took, part of a much larger feast, symbolised a great moment in Israel's history when they were delivered by God from the hand of their oppressors. It was this act of saving grace that gave them their identity and a point of reference. That occasion was the exodus and this continuing celebration meal was a Passover feast.

The meal is reinterpreted by Jesus at the deepest level. Bread and wine stand for his body and his blood, both of which are given to the disciples, broken and poured out for them. The bread of exit has become the bread of entry into the deep, saving forgiveness of God; the wine is now not just a drink of rejoicing but also an embracing of his life, laid down in loving sacrifice.

We cannot but see the shadow of the cross once more, because it is the cross that will make this communion of sharing in precious gifts possible. It is a shared recollection of his life laid down, a tasting of grace and forgiveness, and even, in a way we can never fully comprehend, somehow a receiving of his very self.

In Luke's journey, at this point we come to a new and defining moment. This new 'exodus' is not wrought with the strength that held mighty waters at bay, but reaches out from a piece of wood on which bloodied and nailed arms have been laid. In the dying of Jesus, the flood of heaven's love is loosed, and broken lives are made whole. Here indeed is 'love, vast as the ocean'.

Holy Communion is the celebration of these things. What might assist you, so that you can hold the wonder of his life laid down when you take bread and wine? Is there a fitting response?

ANDY JOHN

Remember me in your kingdom

Then [the criminal] said, 'Jesus, remember me when you come into your kingdom.' He replied, 'Truly I tell you, today you will be with me in Paradise.'

In my chapel, there is a simple piece of wood on to which are carved these words: 'Jesus, remember me when you come into your kingdom.' Whoever stands behind the Communion table will see it. It is a reminder to anyone who reads the words that we have been saved by grace (Ephesians 2:5) and welcomed by a Saviour whose life laid down has won us for God's rich mercy. Christian hymns and poems have captured this extraordinary truth down the ages. Charles Wesley hit the nail on the head in 'O for a thousand tongues to sing': 'He breaks the power of cancelled sin, He sets the prisoner free; His blood can make the foulest clean, His blood availed for me.'

Luke's account at this point is unique. Only here do we read the words of this criminal whose final gasp (we assume) becomes a prayer. By conveying them to us, Luke invites us to see something extraordinary about the boundless love of Jesus. There is no one beyond its reach, none too broken to fix, none too wretched to redeem, none too far gone that they cannot be found and saved. So, we are meant to see the height and depth and breadth of this grace and to marvel at it once more—but not from a distance. Instead, we are invited to identify with this dying man, because we too are in need of the very grace he received and the gentle words of assurance that Jesus will bring us home.

When our consciences whisper destructive thoughts about our failings and broken promises, when we feel utterly wretched, perhaps because of our habitual sinning, and when the future seems bleak to us, these are words meant for us. From the lips of Jesus himself, we are told that those who have found in him their hope and joy stand on a promise that will not fail and ground which will not move.

The criminal found in Jesus something he lacked. His prayer flowed from being near Jesus. Our lives need not be marked by despair but a gentle trust in his secure love.

ANDY JOHN

The follower from afar

Now there was a good and righteous man named Joseph, who, though a member of the council, had not agreed to their plan and action. He came from the Jewish town of Arimathea, and he was waiting expectantly for the kingdom of God. This man went to Pilate and asked for the body of Jesus. Then he took it down, wrapped it in a linen cloth, and laid it in a rock-hewn tomb where no one had ever been laid.

I love the personal stories, the almost tangential moments in the Gospels that seem to lie on the edge of the main plot. Today's passage contains one of these occasions: it is not an essential part of the main story but, nonetheless, it has something important to say.

Luke tells us that there was a good and righteous man named Joseph—a God-fearing believer who distanced himself from the actions of the Sanhedrin even though he was a part of it. He, like faithful Simeon (Luke 2:25–26), was waiting for the kingdom to come. Unlike Simeon, though, he was a 'secret' disciple. His was a fragile, even compromised faith, but it was also one in which the seeds of something strong and good lay.

Luke tells us that Joseph's devotion was strong. He took the body of Jesus down from the cross and tended the dead Christ, presumably becoming unclean himself as a consequence. Luke, however, in telling us this, intends to do more than just link the cross and the resurrection. He shows us that even secret disciples, all those who are on this journey, are people for whom God has a purpose. We may feel that the journey has held similar challenges for us. We have not found it easy to 'own' Jesus, and our progress has been faltering, but we can take from this story the hope that we find grace through our generous God. We can be assured that his work in us will not stumble or cease.

That Joseph is a secret disciple might tempt us to dismiss him, but his story shows us that all who are on this journey find moments when they do extraordinary things. That might mean us, too.

ANDY JOHN

A new day

But on the first day of the week, at early dawn, they came to the tomb, taking the spices that they had prepared. They found the stone rolled away from the tomb, but when they went in, they did not find the body. While they were perplexed about this, suddenly two men in dazzling clothes stood beside them. The women were terrified and bowed their faces to the ground, but the men said to them, 'Why do you look for the living among the dead? He is not here, but has risen.'

Today's part of the journey is sublime and there are two things I want to draw from this passage. The first is that it is the dawning of a new day—literally. It was early and the first day of the week. This particular new dawn also marks the start of a new era: a new created order has dawned, much like the first day recorded in Genesis, and with it come new possibilities for a life lived in the love of God. Paul says something similar to the Corinthian Christians (2 Corinthians 5:17) as he shows that the death and resurrection of Jesus mark an end to the old order of sin and death and a new start for believers.

The second point is the challenge that follows, which is breathtaking: 'Why do you look for the living among the dead?' (v. 5). For Luke, this might be the high point of his Gospel. The challenge requires a complete change in those who hear it—in the women and then all the disciples. We can no longer live as though Christ were not alive, as if the grave has not been robbed of its final power and the future is a matter of random events utterly unconnected to this divine intervention in a tiny corner of the world.

If Jesus' death marks the point at which God's identification with people is most profoundly expressed, the resurrection asserts God's sovereignty over all things. Jesus is made, truly, Lord of all.

The journey the women undertook physically was overshadowed by the journey of faith this event asked of them. How does the risen Jesus call you forward to new trust and obedience?

ANDY JOHN

New heralds and new hope

Now it was Mary Magdalene, Joanna, Mary the mother of James, and the other women with them who told this to the apostles. But these words seemed to them an idle tale, and they did not believe them. But Peter got up and ran to the tomb; stooping and looking in, he saw the linen cloths by themselves; then he went home, amazed at what had happened.

In this second passage from Luke 24, we hear how the women became the first bearers of the good news about the resurrection. Peter's assessment is hardly brimming with understanding and faith as he arrives. Do these events have significance beyond being simple descriptions of what took place and, if they do, in what sense?

Many have seen a strong affirmation of the place of women in both ministry and the purposes of God in this sequence. Jesus had always shown himself to the outcast, the marginalised and frail, and there is no doubt that his appearance to the women is in keeping with this revelation. The message of resurrection is given to some of the least significant people in his society, whose testimony would not even be recognised in court. This is important, because Jesus always comes to such people. His welcoming love seeks out those who feel they have nothing and are of no value. This astonishing privilege underscores how Christ sees them and treasures them and loves them, and that is gospel hope.

Peter, too, in a rather muted and uncertain manner, has something to say to us. He arrives at the tomb and analyses what he sees, without appearing to grasp what has taken place. For him, the full truth will become clear a little later in the day. His visit to the tomb is important also because it shows that signs and pointers count for little if there is no encounter with Jesus himself. It is this meeting that brings about a living resurrection faith. The evidence can point and invite questions, wonder and reflection, but only a personal encounter with the living Christ can open the door to true faith.

The message that Jesus was alive came unexpectedly and shows that encountering him is at the heart of living faith. What does this mean for you?

ANDY JOHN

Ruined hopes?

'But we had hoped that he was the one to redeem Israel. Yes, and besides all this, it is now the third day since these things took place.'

We might describe the walk to Emmaus as long and winding, and note that the inner journey is more significant than the physical one undertaken here. This is so rich a passage on which to reflect that just one verse will suffice for today.

So we join our sojourners as they walk. Jesus has drawn alongside them as they pour out their woes to an uninvited, but seemingly welcome, guest. They do not recognise him because they are kept, at this time, from seeing who he is (v. 16). Their woes are fed by their ruined hopes and expectations. Whatever else the cross and death of Jesus meant, it was most certainly not the triumph of God, the high point and end of all that Jesus had come to achieve. For these disciples it meant nothing other than the end of the adventure and the destruction of their future.

The disciples show us how quickly Jesus has become a figure of the past: 'We had hoped', they say, 'that he was the one to redeem Israel' (v. 21). Their meaning is clear. Jesus might have been the one to roll back the invaders, restore the nation's fortunes, re-animate the covenant and secure the reign of David's son for all time. But now it is gone. All of it.

Stepping into the shoes of these disciples might help us relate to their story. We may have carried dashed hopes, believing that the future was strewn with uncertainty and despair. We might even have felt, as did they, that Jesus was a figure from a past long emptied of joy and purpose. This is not the end of the story, though, and faith born again when eyes are unblinded takes us beyond the losses and sadness. Hope comes when we meet him as the one who died for us, but is now alive.

The despair of the disciples on the way to Emmaus is understandable.
Thinking of difficult times in your life, how does this story
speak to you afresh?

ANDY JOHN

103

Jesus the inspired teacher

Then beginning with Moses and all the prophets, he interpreted to them the things about himself in all the scriptures.

The patience of Jesus with these and all the disciples is probably something we rarely ponder. I wonder how many times he has whispered into my own deaf ears the same message again and again and again! In today's passage, we hear how he begins to teach these frail disciples about himself, using the scriptures to restore their damaged faith.

The way in which Jesus teaches them is significant. He refers to the scriptures that bear witness to him from Moses through to the prophets. In other words, he draws the biblical lines together to show them the bigger picture. All these things were not accidents, not beyond the purposes of God; in fact, they demonstrate that God is Lord of all. The resurrection is itself the culmination of all his good and loving purposes. This continuity with everything done under the first covenant shows both God's lordship and his faithfulness. It puts straight the distorted view that the disciples were holding. It is almost as though he unpicks the damaged threads and weaves a more faithful account of God and his steadfastness across the ages. Sometimes the teacher needs to undo, as well as recreate, in order for truth to be established.

We need to bring this truth alongside the earlier passages we have read, about encountering Jesus. We need both his word and his Spirit in our lives. Meeting Christ and allowing him to shape us through his word sit together. Too often, the church—Christians like you and me—has majored on one aspect of his ministry to us and so has become unbalanced. If we are incapable of being taught by him, we are incapable of continuing the journey a little further. The disciples show us that there is no need to become stuck, paralysed by circumstances, doubts and fears, because our saving, risen teacher is at hand and he can be trusted.

The way in which Jesus draws faith from his followers can speak to us afresh. He is our best teacher as he knows the way ahead. Can we see how he shapes our lives by his word?

ANDY JOHN

Burning hearts

Then their eyes were opened, and they recognised him; and he vanished from their sight. They said to each other, 'Were not our hearts burning within us while he was talking to us on the road, while he was opening the scriptures to us?'

I have in my study a picture of today's reading by the artist Caravaggio—sadly, not the original! It is called *The Supper at Emmaus* and captures the moment when Jesus is recognised by these two disciples. There are actually two such paintings by Caravaggio. This one, the more famous, is lighter and throws the characters further forward in a more dramatic way than the darker, though also profound, depiction. Here, the disciples are frozen in a moment of shock, articles on the table have been disturbed and the facial expressions all combine to highlight the drama of recognition. Jesus is their guest. The dead Christ is alive and at their side!

Luke captures in words not only the drama but also its impact on the disciples. Their eyes have been opened and they understand why their hearts were 'burning' on the road. They cannot contain their excitement and set off for Jerusalem immediately.

That moment of drama might have been unique, but we can relate to the disciples' excitement and incredulity. When we meet with Jesus there can be a profound change in us. Such meetings might be in a quiet moment of prayer, in church, on the street or in a shop. The everyday is suddenly blessed by an extraordinary moment of closeness. We know Jesus is at our side. We see him, too—if not physically, then with our inward eyes—and our hearts cannot feel indifferent to the encounter. These are moments to cherish and they hold us steady when more arid or difficult times come. They give us trust when the river of grace seems to have run dry. Having faith like that is how we continue the journey—always open and seeking the one whose presence stirs us.

Jesus withheld their recognising him until this moment, perhaps to heighten its impact on them. Encounters like this deepen and renew our passion and love for him. Have you reflected on the way blessing sustains our faith?

ANDY JOHN

Hands and feet, in beauty glorified

He said to them, 'Why are you frightened, and why do doubts arise in your hearts? Look at my hands and my feet; see that it is I myself. Touch me and see; for a ghost does not have flesh and bones as you see that I have.' And when he had said this, he showed them his hands and his feet.

When the Emmaus disciples arrive in Jerusalem, barely a moment has passed before their words give way to something much like the experience at the inn when they were resting. Jesus appears, speaks words of peace to them and reassures them it really is him. To show it convincingly, he invites them to touch him, much as he did Thomas (John 20:26–27). He shows them the very hands and feet that had been pierced and nailed. Although we are not told this explicitly, it is hard to believe that Luke included these details for any other reason.

There are perhaps two elements to this incident. The first is that Jesus wants his disciples to believe beyond any doubt. The physicality of his approach has this aim in mind. The connection between the earthly body of Jesus and the risen Lord has now been made, which means that this is all real and not imagined.

The second element is that the wounds remain. The piercing has not been removed or healed; when he ascends into heaven, those very wounds will go with him. I wonder how familiar you are with the great hymn 'Crown him with many crowns' by Matthew Bridges, and the line that reads, 'those wounds yet visible above, in beauty glorified'. Here is the extraordinary truth about the risen Jesus: he takes what was marred by human hands, fully redeemed, into highest heaven. Those marks of suffering and pain go there too. Is it any wonder he understands our every weakness and agony? He has experienced it himself and it remains a part of him, even when dying and death can happen no more.

The disciples were terrified when they met Jesus, but the sheer physical nature of his encounter with them means that we, too, have a share in something that is physical as well as spiritual. What are the implications of this?

ANDY JOHN

The blessedness of departure

While he was blessing them, he withdrew from them and was carried up into heaven. And they worshipped him, and returned to Jerusalem with great joy; and they were continually in the temple blessing God.

Departures are rarely welcomed or seen positively. We only need to witness the tears of farewell at any airport to get a sense of what leaving loved ones means. This marks a huge contrast with the experience of the disciples after Jesus' ascension: we are told that they were continually in the temple blessing God (v. 53). They appear to have welcomed his going as essentially good news. Why is this?

First, Jesus prepared them for a blessing to come that would be limitless (v. 49). The tasks they were now to undertake would be done with the strength of the very one whom they had followed, loved and served. What brought them joy was bearing good news to all the world. Second, I wonder if they understood that his going really was a final crowning moment. He had achieved all that the Father had sent him to do and was now returning to God. As he blessed them, it was no longer as the suffering Son of Man but as the Christ, risen with healing in his wings.

This incident marks the completion of Luke's retelling of the story of Jesus' journey, at least in relation to his earthly ministry. We began with a crowd welcoming him, albeit fleetingly, and end with a crowd whose devotion will not fail and a cause that will lead them out on new adventures and sometimes out on to choppy waters.

This is the extraordinary story of Luke's journey and, because we find ourselves reading it even today, we are included in it, too. Like the disciples, we are called to make Jesus known and bring good news to all the earth. When we feel our own weaknesses, we can recall the wounds Jesus bears; when we feel overwhelmed by doubts and troubles, we can recall his coming to the disciples on the Emmaus road, walking so patiently until their eyes were opened and their hearts burned.

The journey from Palm Sunday to Easter marks a movement towards hope and joy. How can this story invite you to travel in the same direction?

ANDY JOHN

Raised in glory: 1 Corinthians 15

'In the beginning… God…' (Genesis 1:1). The resurrection begins and ends with God. There might be different responses to questions beginning 'Why?' or 'How?', but the answer to 'Who?' is always God.

Paul is writing to a group of Christians who had idolised leaders, followed the latest spiritual fashion without testing it, and forgotten that conversion to Christ involved every area of life, including intimate relationships, what they ate and how they conducted themselves in worship. Now they were questioning whether or not Jesus was raised from death and what the resurrection might look like. Paul resists the temptation to focus on sin and why Jesus died—in some ways these are easier issues to tackle. Instead, the whole chapter looks at the resurrection—what happened after Jesus died and was buried.

The issue of the resurrection is both weighty and wonderful. In these weeks after Easter, as we again consume chocolate or alcohol or begin to have more screentime after the abstinence we practised during Lent, we might say the words, 'Christ is risen' without thinking about them. How, though, exactly, is the resurrection good news? Why do physical bodies matter before and after death?

The question of the good news arises at different points in this chapter, while the nature of resurrection (and other) bodies is dealt with towards the end. As I have read this passage and written the following notes, I have become conscious of the variety of bodies around me. I am acutely aware of family and friends whose physical bodies are deteriorating, with significant consequences. Part of the challenge of this chapter has been to discover what the good news and resurrection mean in my daily life. On every occasion, I have been brought back to God—sometimes in repentance, sometimes in awe, always with thankfulness. There are no easy answers, but God remains powerful and loving as we wrestle with such questions.

I encourage you to read the chapter in one sitting and, if you have time, read the whole letter to the Corinthians to put it in context and enrich your understanding and prayer. Finally, if you want to take your studies further, I recommend Anthony Thiselton's *The First Epistle to the Corinthians* (Eerdmans, 2013), which brings this chapter to life.

LAKSHMI JEFFREYS

Be careful with good news

Now I should remind you, brothers and sisters, of the good news that I proclaimed to you, which you in turn received, in which also you stand, through which also you are being saved, if you hold firmly to the message that I proclaimed to you—unless you have come to believe in vain. For I handed on to you as of first importance what I in turn had received...

Listening to the radio one morning, our then nine-year-old voiced a question that many adults wonder about: 'Why is the news always bad?' Even apparently positive stories are given a negative 'spin' so that we remain in a state of fear or disbelief at how terrible 'they' are or the world is. The irony is that much of what we hear has little, if any, real impact on us, whether it is about a distant war or famine or a burglary in the next town. We simply feel scared, angry or sad.

God turns the ways of the world upside down. In a society used to doing what an individual wants because no one else really cares, Paul tells the Corinthians again that he is a herald of good news. His message puts everything into perspective and actually makes a difference to any who truly latch on to it. Unlike the news on the radio, God's good news will transform the lives of all who continue to hold firm.

Paul is talking about more than agreeing in theory that God can save. He points out that the Corinthians are in a state of being saved, as they act on what they have heard and experienced. There is a need to both recognise the facts Paul has shared and live them out. Just as Paul handed to the Corinthians what he had received, so the people of this church need to allow truth about God to transform their existence. This is not a hasty, brief commitment before moving on to the next good idea. Details of the message will come later. For now, God's good news is the bedrock of everything and will revolutionise reality for all who believe.

Pray that God's good news impacts those directly affected by other news.

LAKSHMI JEFFREYS

Evidence of good news

… that Christ died for our sins in accordance with the scriptures, and that he was buried, and that he was raised on the third day in accordance with the scriptures, and that he appeared to Cephas, then to the twelve. Then he appeared to more than five hundred brothers and sisters at one time, most of whom are still alive, though some have died.

We now come to the details of the good news to which Paul has been referring. Jesus Christ died for our sins; he was buried; he was raised on the third day; he appeared to named individuals and to several others, some of whom were still around, and this was foretold in the scriptures.

Each element of this good news is worth pondering. First, Jesus' death was for a purpose and had an impact on every person who has ever lived as he died for our sins, according to God's will, which the scriptures said would be the case. The statement that Jesus' body was buried highlights the reality of his death and the miracle involved in a dead body being raised to life. Jesus' resurrection occurred on the third day, as the scriptures had prophesied—again demonstrating that this was an act of God. Jesus then appeared to Peter (Cephas), of whom the Corinthians had heard (1 Corinthians 1:12 and 9:5). No one today can prove when and how Jesus appeared to the 500, but, at the time, the Corinthians would have been able to verify that statement.

Yesterday, we saw that it is possible to hear news without it making an impact on how we live. Today, Paul reminds us, as he reminded the Corinthians, that Jesus' resurrection was both foretold in what we know as the Old Testament and there were people who had experienced the risen Lord. In other words, this news is personal as well as historical and global. To understand what we have heard, however, we need the scriptural context of God's revelation, promises, judgement and grace. Jesus' resurrection makes increasing sense and becomes transformational as we discover, via the Old Testament as well as this letter, how it confirms and continues God's dealings with the world.

Slowly pray through a Christian creed.

LAKSHMI JEFFREYS

God's grace is for all

Then he appeared to James, then to all the apostles. Last of all, as to someone untimely born, he appeared also to me. For I am the least of the apostles, unfit to be called an apostle, because I persecuted the church of God. But by the grace of God I am what I am, and his grace towards me has not been in vain. On the contrary, I worked harder than any of them—though it was not I, but the grace of God that is with me. Whether then it was I or they, so we proclaim and so you have come to believe.

Paul can appear extraordinarily harsh on himself. The words 'someone untimely born' are more accurately and graphically translated as 'a miscarried foetus'. At the end of a list of significant people to whom Jesus appeared after God raised him from death, Paul finally includes himself—someone who was born not fully formed, who persecuted the church and had not spent time with Jesus during his ministry on earth. Paul is writing to people who were in danger of idolising leaders and teachers (see Introduction), so he apparently denigrates himself as he offers God's view. It is as if he is saying, 'God is so generous and forgiving that Jesus appeared even to a lesser human specimen such as I, and I have shared this message of transforming love and grace with you.'

As mentioned earlier, it is important to read this passage in the context of the whole letter. Paul is not demonstrating a serious lack of self-worth. Neither does he need to prove himself to his hearers. Instead, he wants them to know God's grace—God's love and mercy, supremely shown in the life, death and resurrection of Jesus. It does not matter what we have done in the past or how zealous we are for God now. Anything wrong can be transformed by God's grace; anything right is a result of God's grace. We matter because of who God is and what God does.

If God accepts all I have done in the past and how I am now, can I accept myself and allow God's grace to transform me?

LAKSHMI JEFFREYS

111

Beyond imagination

Now if Christ is proclaimed as raised from the dead, how can some of you say there is no resurrection of the dead? If there is no resurrection of the dead, then Christ has not been raised; and if Christ has not been raised, then our proclamation has been in vain and your faith has been in vain.

A number of years ago, I stayed with a family in East Africa. The mother had lived her whole life in the country and understood its climate well. When the temperature was about 15°C, she appeared in thick socks, a heavy jumper and a knitted hat. She was shocked to see me in a short-sleeved dress and could not believe that I was not cold. I explained that sometimes the temperature in England fell below 0°C, to which she responded, 'So you don't go out?' When I described how we just wrapped up warm and got on with life, she exclaimed, 'But you would die!' She was unable to imagine anyone surviving temperatures so far below the conditions that she experienced as life-threateningly cold!

Perhaps there were people in the church at Corinth who simply could not imagine resurrection. Because the concept was beyond anything they could hold in mind, it could not exist. Paul refutes this utterly. The whole of the gospel depends on Christ having been raised from the dead. Jesus was raised first, and, in time, all believers will be raised from death. If Christ has not been raised, there is absolutely no basis for Christian faith. Everything Paul has preached and the Corinthians have believed is empty, hollow. As one person said, 'No one can give himself to a dead man; no one can expect anything or receive anything from a dead man.'

Resurrection goes beyond human imagination to God's action. The whole Bible tells of God's activities, primarily to restore his relationship with humanity. In this context, raising Jesus from death is no longer limited by what we might imagine. Instead, resurrection becomes a cause for faith and rejoicing, particularly as we discover how, one day, all Christians will experience what we can barely dream of.

Is God bigger or smaller than your imagination?

LAKSHMI JEFFREYS

Faith in God

We are even found to be misrepresenting God, because we testified of God that he raised Christ—whom he did not raise if it is true that the dead are not raised. For if the dead are not raised, then Christ has not been raised. If Christ has not been raised, your faith is futile and you are still in your sins. Then those also who have died in Christ have perished. If for this life only we have hoped in Christ, we are of all people most to be pitied.

'Where does God fit?' It might help the church today if more people asked and answered this question. Many organisations demand a correct profession of faith, particular lifestyles, inclusion or, perhaps, even exclusion of particular individuals or groups, but it is hard to know where God fits. Others will speak about living according to 'Christian' values, when in fact they are speaking of values identical to those of anyone (regardless of religious faith) whose moral code includes, for example, not stealing, lying or cheating.

For Paul, the question of where God fits is central. Resurrection is not simply a theory to which Christians must assent, something we must believe at all costs. It is about God. It was God who raised Jesus from death. If God did not do this, then people are in a state of sin—putting self before God with no way of changing their situation. There is no forgiveness, no opportunity for transforming their lives, nothing after death. This leads us to the final sentence: if there is no resurrection, then Christians can only be objects of pity—delusional, sad and with nothing to hope for.

There is a danger that some people justify faith in God by saying that we can only accept the resurrection if we have faith. Then, if Jesus' body were produced, Christian faith would be debunked. Faith is more robust than that: it is a gift from God and results in transformed lives.

Faith in the God whose love is stronger than death is a weighty issue. Perhaps we can pray as we consider the evidence, read the Bible, discuss with others and reflect on experience—then see what happens.

Slowly pray through Psalm 131.

LAKSHMI JEFFREYS

One for all

But in fact Christ has been raised from the dead, the first fruits of those who have died. For since death came through a human being, the resurrection of the dead has also come through a human being; for as all die in Adam, so all will be made alive in Christ. But each in his own order: Christ the first fruits, then at his coming those who belong to Christ.

After questioning and uncertainty, there is a sigh of relief as we read the opening words of today's passage. The point is that God has raised Jesus Christ from the dead. We can argue and worry as much as we want to about what life would be like if this were not the case, but, as the Christian faith proclaims the resurrection of Jesus, resurrection is possible. Jesus' resurrection is likened to the first crop of the harvest—a sign of all that is to come. Jesus was raised first, and when Jesus comes again, all Christians who have died will be raised.

There is a shift in emphasis from death to life, and this life is not simply for God's people of the Old Testament but for the whole world. There is a reminder that Jesus' resurrection is for everyone, just as sin committed immediately after God created the world resulted in all people sinning. This is not easy for us to understand. So much of our life is focused on us as individuals that this idea of 'belonging' with others is less familiar, perhaps, than it would have been in former times.

Theologian Anthony Thiselton suggests an analogy that might help us understand this better. In a football match, when one person gives away a penalty or someone scores a goal, the whole team is affected. An individual's action has influenced everyone for good or ill, because they belong to one team.

Paul stated earlier in the letter that Christians are the body of Christ. As a result of the resurrection, we can show that we belong to Christ, with him as the head, or we can continue to behave as if we belong to Adam. Faith and trust in God determine the outcome.

'We are all one in Christ Jesus. We belong to him through faith.'
What does this mean?

LAKSHMI JEFFREYS

All shall be well

Then comes the end, when [Jesus] hands over the kingdom to God the
Father, after he has destroyed every ruler and every authority and power.
For he must reign until he has put all his enemies under his feet. The
last enemy to be destroyed is death. For 'God has put all things in subjection under his feet.' But when it says, 'All things are put in subjection', it is plain that this does not include the one who put all things in
subjection under him. When all things are subjected to him, then the
Son himself will also be subjected to the one who put all things in subjection under him, so that God may be all in all.

At the beginning of the chapter, the focus was on good news. Perhaps
now we are hearing the best news. Everything that destroys will itself
ultimately be destroyed (a better translation is 'annihilated'), including
death. Jesus will reign with all things in subjection to him and God will
be recognised as God.

One of the habits in Stephen Covey's book 7 *Habits of Highly Effective
People* is to 'begin with the end in mind'. If we know what we are working—or even living—for, we are far more likely to experience it. When
learning to drive a car, a good student will listen carefully to the instruc-
tor, not simply to learn particular skills but also with the aim of becoming a proficient driver. With a focus on being a careful independent
driver, such a learner is more likely to pass a driving test than someone
who concentrates on individual skills only.

Today's Bible passage spells out what the end will be like. In the
words of the mystic Julian of Norwich, 'all manner of thing shall be well'.
God, who raised Jesus from death, will be recognised as the source and
creator of all. Jesus will have completed the work of the Father in the
power of the Spirit so that Christians can worship God who is all in all.
With the end in mind, we can learn to worship God using the Bible,
church, sacraments, traditions and other aids to faith without inadvert-
ently putting them in God's place.

What are your idols (things or people that you worship instead of God)?

LAKSHMI JEFFREYS

Peer pressure

And why are we putting ourselves in danger every hour? I die every day! That is as certain, brothers and sisters, as my boasting of you—a boast that I make in Christ Jesus our Lord. If with merely human hopes I fought with wild animals at Ephesus, what would I have gained by it? If the dead are not raised, 'Let us eat and drink, for tomorrow we die.' Do not be deceived: 'Bad company ruins good morals.' Come to a sober and right mind, and sin no more; for some people have no knowledge of God. I say this to your shame.

What is the point? This is not necessarily a question the Corinthians asked Paul, but he answers it anyway. If death is the end, there is absolutely no point to anything Paul has done for the Christian church—and, by this stage, he has endured significant suffering and some near-death experiences. If he went through all of this employing only human endurance and resources, no good would come of it for anyone. If death is the end, then there is no purpose in living other than for the self. Why not do what everyone else does and hang the consequences?

Sadly, there are many Christians who forget God and adopt this lifestyle. The businessman who was unfaithful to his wife at a conference, for example, and eventually left his family for the other woman, ignored God's power and love, supremely demonstrated in the resurrection. As we have seen, if God raised Jesus from death, then there is always the possibility of forgiveness and hope.

Magazines, television and other forms of media are crammed with articles about improving life. Most of them focus on inner strength, just occasionally recognising the importance of supportive friends and family. The resurrection changes the focus from self to God and brings not just improved life, but the best life with God for eternity.

Loving God, forgive me for losing perspective and forgetting that resurrection is about your love, forgiveness and grace. Thank you that you have demonstrated power to overcome death so there is nothing too big to transform in individuals' lives or the whole world. Grant me courage to hold on to you and not give in to society's pressure to live for self.

LAKSHMI JEFFREYS

Questions and pictures

But someone will ask, 'How are the dead raised? With what kind of body do they come?' Fool! What you sow does not come to life unless it dies. And as for what you sow, you do not sow the body that is to be, but a bare seed, perhaps of wheat or of some other grain. But God gives it a body as he has chosen, and to each kind of seed its own body. Not all flesh is alike, but there is one flesh for human beings, another for animals, another for birds, and another for fish.

'But I don't want to spend forever sitting on a cloud in a white dress playing a harp!' Several years ago a fun-loving friend shared her objections to Christian faith and, particularly, her perception of heaven and post-resurrection existence. I resisted the temptation to ask where on earth she had gained such a daft idea and agreed that the picture she presented was boring, adding that it did not fit with what was written in the Bible. Like many people, my friend had developed notions based more on fancy than fact.

My Greek is limited, but I wonder if Paul's response to the question about resurrection bodies is effectively, 'You are speaking utter twaddle!' All we need to do is look at the world around us to see that bodies are all different, depending on their nature, age and stage of life. The body of a seed is utterly unrecognisable when it becomes wheat. The same body changes over time: the woman in her 80s looks nothing like she did in a photograph when she was four years old. Meanwhile, our puppy is outside chasing blackbirds: their bodies are not even similar!

All of us have questions about faith, but, in time, we might discover that we do not always need answers in order to trust God. Paul tells the Corinthians that details of the resurrection—in this case, what their bodies will look like—are less important than the author of our resurrection, who designed all bodies.

We praise you, God, for the beauty and diversity of all the bodies you have created.

LAKSHMI JEFFREYS

Before and after resurrection

There are both heavenly bodies and earthly bodies, but the glory of the heavenly is one thing, and that of the earthly is another... So it is with the resurrection of the dead. What is sown is perishable, what is raised is imperishable. It is sown in dishonour, it is raised in glory. It is sown in weakness, it is raised in power. It is sown a physical body, it is raised a spiritual body. If there is a physical body, there is also a spiritual body.

There is awe and wonder as Paul continues to explain the magnificence of resurrection. Jesus came to earth as a bodily human, who died, but, when God raised him from the dead, his body was transformed. Paul uses four statements to describe the transformation:

- The earthly body decays—it is perishable (anyone over 40 will attest to this!)—but the resurrection body will reverse decay, so that in God's presence there will be full life.
- The earthly body is sown in dishonour: it is subject to sin. The resurrection body is subject to glory, radiance, sinlessness.
- The earthly body is sown in weakness. It is in a particular time and place and thereby limited. The resurrection body is raised in power. This is not to say that Christians become superheroes after death: this power is the ability to carry out God's will, empowered by the Holy Spirit.
- The earthly body is physical. The resurrection body is spiritual—that is, infused with the Holy Spirit rather than ethereal.

The key issue for Paul is that we have a body for our existence on earth and, when God brings about the resurrection, he will provide a suitable body for existence with him in eternity. Life in all its fullness will be experienced by bodies that are sinless, Spirit-filled and recognisably from God. God will be 'all in all' (v. 28).

While resurrection bodies will be different from earthly bodies, can we experience something of the presence and power of the Holy Spirit in our (decaying) bodies?

LAKSHMI JEFFREYS

Family likeness

Thus it is written, 'The first man, Adam, became a living being'; the last Adam became a life-giving spirit. But it is not the spiritual that is first, but the physical, and then the spiritual. The first man was from the earth, a man of dust; the second man is from heaven. As was the man of dust, so are those who are of the dust; and as is the man of heaven, so are those who are of heaven. Just as we have borne the image of the man of dust, we will also bear the image of the man of heaven.

Adam is not only the name of the first created person but also the name that Paul uses to refer to humanity. Hence the 'first Adam' is our ancestor and represents all people before salvation, while the 'last Adam' is Jesus. As Anthony Thiselton says, Jesus is the head and representative of the new humanity and new order of being. Once again, Paul contrasts the physical and the spiritual, reminding his hearers that the old order was mortal and those in Christ pertain to heaven.

There are practical implications, to which Paul alludes at the end of the passage. Just as we have lived as sinful people in the likeness of Adam, so, in Christ, we also bear the image of God. Sometimes in family photographs, the resemblance between parents, children and siblings is striking. More interesting is when not only are there physical similarities but members of the same family also have similar mannerisms, turns of phrase and even ways of approaching particular incidents in life. During a church service, two-year-old Max (not his real name) was sitting with his grandparents who were visiting. It was fascinating to see how the grandfather interacted with Max in an almost identical manner to that of Max's dad, gently and kindly. Family likeness went beyond facial resemblance here to include life-enhancing character traits.

Christians bear the image of Christ and that can include demonstrating the fruit of the Spirit (Galatians 5:22–23). Do we pray to the God of resurrection to grow his image within us?

May we faithfully bear the image of the living God, so that we and all around us catch glimpses of true life.

LAKSHMI JEFFREYS

Yet more good news!

What I am saying, brothers and sisters, is this: flesh and blood cannot inherit the kingdom of God, nor does the perishable inherit the imperishable. Listen, I will tell you a mystery! We will not all die, but we will all be changed, in a moment, in the twinkling of an eye, at the last trumpet. For the trumpet will sound, and the dead will be raised imperishable, and we will be changed.

When people are profiled—for example, in national publications or, in the case of a local school, the weekly newsletter—important information is set out about the individual's area of work or interest. At the end, there might be an item of trivia, such as a response to, 'Tell us a secret.' Answers have revealed people who floss daily, once learned the saxophone or have a fear of spiders. None of this is important to daily life, but it is a source of amusement or curiosity.

The same is true of Paul's statement, 'Listen, I will tell you a mystery!' (v. 51). It is as if Paul is about to tell the Corinthians a secret such as those mentioned above, at the end of a letter containing essential, life-giving material. The Corinthians need to understand that there is a bodily resurrection given by God. Not to recognise this is to deny the gospel.

Paul's argument in the last few verses has been that there are two kinds of bodies: one for earthly living, a sinful body which decays over time, and a resurrection body, imbued with the Holy Spirit, which exudes the life of God. 'Flesh and blood' (v. 50) refers to those who are not in Christ, all who have not experienced resurrection life. Anyone who has not undergone resurrection cannot inherit the kingdom of God.

Next he tells them something almost for fun. Transformation will take place in a flash, both for those who have died and for those who are still alive when Jesus comes again. A trumpet will sound (presumably blown by an angel or archangel) and everyone will be changed. Paul will continue with important information about death, but for now there is almost an injection of light relief.

Praise God for unnecessary details of good news!

LAKSHMI JEFFREYS

Not the final frontier

For this perishable body must put on imperishability, and this mortal body must put on immortality. When this perishable body puts on imper- ishability, and this mortal body puts on immortality, then the saying that is written will be fulfilled: 'Death has been swallowed up in victory.' 'Where, O death, is your victory? Where, O death, is your sting?'

At the end, the body that decays will be replaced by one which will never wear out, and human nature, subject to death, will be trans- formed into one which cannot be touched by death. Earlier in the letter (v. 26), Paul talked about death as the final enemy to be overthrown. Here, he recites verses mocking death: it has no more power; Christ has the victory; the sting of death, sin, has gone.

The image of death being 'swallowed' (v. 54) is wonderful because it reminds us of how much bigger God is than death. Some people will be fans of the *Star Trek* television series and films. The opening lines include the words, 'Space, the final frontier… [our] mission: to explore strange new worlds, to seek out new life and new civilisations, to boldly go where no man has gone before.' As these words are spoken, the accomp- anying images of space are vast, endless and potentially terrifying.

Death, for many people, is not a final frontier; it is simply final. It is vast, endless and terrifying, whether someone faces his or her own death or the death of a loved one. Yet, Paul says here that death has been swal- lowed up in victory. It is no longer the end, because of God's love and grace, shown primarily in his raising Jesus from death and, ultimately, raising from death all those in Christ.

This side of heaven, we experience the effects of death—grief, sad- ness, fear and other feelings resulting from sin. The hope of resurrection does not diminish death, but offers us perspective: God is bigger than death. We can trust God with all our feelings and fears about death because God is more powerful than death. God has raised Jesus from death so that we can boldly go where Jesus *has* gone before.

For Christians, death is not the end but the beginning.

LAKSHMI JEFFREYS

So what?

The sting of death is sin, and the power of sin is the law. But thanks be to God, who gives us the victory through our Lord Jesus Christ. Therefore, my beloved, be steadfast, immovable, always excelling in the work of the Lord, because you know that in the Lord your labour is not in vain.

Paul ends his magnificent treatise on death and resurrection in a practical manner. Yesterday, we recognised that the emotional response to death is usually fear, grief and sadness as a result of sin. Today, we are reminded of the theological reason for this: sin is made known via the law. Paul examines this link more fully in his letters to the Romans and the Galatians, but for now he assumes that sin results from breaking God's law. The penalty for sin is death, 'But thanks be to God, who gives us the victory through our Lord Jesus Christ' (v. 57).

We have now come full circle in this chapter. At the beginning, Paul reminded his hearers of good news from God. He ends with thanksgiving for God's victory over sin and death through the resurrection of Jesus—the substance of the good news he first proclaimed. Just as at the beginning we saw that good news made an impact, so Paul offers the Corinthians practical application of the theory he has expounded.

As God has raised Jesus from death, and death ultimately will have no power, Christians can stay firm in their faith in God. 'The work of the Lord' (v. 58) is to offer the love Paul describes in chapter 13 within and beyond the Christian community. At this point Paul refers to the Corinthians as his beloved.

Constantly showing God's love, regardless of the response, can feel relentlessly demanding. Paul has expressed this and Jesus died to prove it, but if God's love is so powerful that it triumphs even over death, then we who are in Christ can remain loyal and unwavering. We are urged to excel in showing love, reminded that nothing we offer in Jesus' name will be wasted. Resurrection is physical and has practical applications to build up God's people and show God's love to the wider world.

Thanks be to God!

LAKSHMI JEFFREYS

1 and 2 Thessalonians

The birth of the church in Thessalonica is described for us in Acts 17:1–8. Paul followed his usual pattern of preaching in the synagogue, explaining from the scriptures that Jesus was the Messiah. The response was good, with some of the Jews believing, as well as a large number of God-fearing Greeks and quite a few prominent women.

The impression given in Acts is that his mission in Thessalonica lasted three weeks at most (Acts 17:2), but his letters suggest a much longer ministry (perhaps two to three months) during which he preached beyond the synagogue and saw many pagan Greeks being converted as well (1 Thessalonians 1:7–9).

Despite this successful beginning, opposition soon came along when some of the leaders, jealous of Paul's effectiveness, stirred up a riot against him and his team, accusing them of being troublemakers. 'These men who have turned the world upside down have come here as well,' they cried. 'They are preaching against Caesar's rule, saying there is another king, Jesus' (Acts 17:6–7, paraphrased).

Paul and Silas could not be found by the authorities, but Jason and some of the other brothers were dragged before the city officials. Realising that the apostles were in danger, the believers advised them to leave, so they left during the night for Berea.

Paul, of course, was anxious for news of the fledgling church, so sent Timothy to them to see how they were doing. His first letter to the Thessalonian church was probably written from Corinth about AD52, after Timothy returned with news (Acts 18:5). The second letter was probably written a short while later when further news reached the apostle. These epistles are therefore among the earliest of his writings, and reflect his deep love for this group of new believers living in the midst of a hostile environment.

These two brief epistles speak to us in a number of ways: they show the grace and power of God at work in bringing the church into being; they illustrate the characteristics of true Christian ministry; they remind us that believers are called to holy living and suffering is inevitable for those who follow Jesus; they give us a broader perspective on life, teaching us to look for the coming of Jesus again to this world.

TONY HORSFALL

123

A good foundation

We always thank God for all of you and continually mention you in our prayers. We remember before our God and Father your work produced by faith, your labour prompted by love, and your endurance inspired by hope in our Lord Jesus Christ. For we know, brothers and sisters loved by God, that he has chosen you, because our gospel came to you not simply with words but also with power, with the Holy Spirit and deep conviction.

Paul was aware that his ministry in Thessalonica was effective not because of his own cleverness or skill but because God was at work calling the people himself. The evidence of their genuine conversion was clearly seen in their faith, love and hope. Such transformation of life is made possible only by the deep convicting work of the Holy Spirit.

Faith came first. The people believed the message they heard from Paul and responded to it by turning towards God in repentance. For some that meant acknowledging Jesus as the Messiah, for others leaving behind their idolatrous ways, but, for all, it meant identifying with the new community of believers in Thessalonica.

Then came love. True conversion lifts us out of our own small worlds and motivates us to care for others and share the good news with them. This was certainly true in Thessalonica, where the new believers formed themselves into a loving community (1 Thessalonians 4:9–10) from which the gospel message radiated (1 Thessalonians 1:8).

Finally, there was hope. In the midst of opposition and difficulty, these new believers found strength to endure because they believed that Jesus was king and he would one day return in victory. They had a future perspective that gave them strength for their present trials.

I first heard the gospel message as a 14-year-old boy. It came to me with great conviction—exposing my sinfulness, but showing me how to find forgiveness in Jesus. It changed my life, so that faith, love and hope have been at work in me ever since. That can be your experience, too.

Lord, may I receive the gospel message not as merely human words
but also as the word of God.

TONY HORSFALL

Promising beginnings

The Lord's message rang out from you not only in Macedonia and Achaia—your faith in God has become known everywhere. Therefore we do not need to say anything about it, for they themselves report what kind of reception you gave us. They tell how you turned to God from idols to serve the living and true God, and to wait for his Son from heaven, whom he raised from the dead—Jesus, who rescues us from the coming wrath.

Paul and Silas arrived in Thessalonica having been imprisoned in Philippi because of the radical nature of their message (Acts 16:20). Uproar seemed to follow them everywhere, but in Thessalonica they experienced a good reception, at least initially. Many inhabitants of the city embraced the gospel enthusiastically and the story of their conversion spread throughout the region. Here we can see how the gospel message touched them in the past, the present and the future.

First, for the pagan Greeks, it meant a turning away from the idolatry that had characterised their worship previously. Long-held allegiances to false deities had to be given up—a costly choice, involving family opposition and personal upheaval, made possible by a new awareness of a God who was both living and true.

Second, it involved a new outlook on life, choosing to serve the God whom Paul had preached to them, revealed in the person of Jesus. Such a remarkable turnabout, from self-centred living to a life of service, is a mark of true conversion and evidence of a genuine work of God.

Third, it gave them a new perspective on life: they could now look with anticipation to the future in the knowledge that the risen Jesus would one day return to earth. Paul seems to have especially emphasised the second coming to the Thessalonians, and it seems that the imminent return of Jesus as king gave particular hope to these early believers, who often found themselves persecuted and victimised.

We pause today to examine our own spiritual foundations. Have we turned from the 'false gods' in our lives? Do we have a desire to serve God and other people? Is the hope of Jesus' return burning brightly in our hearts?

TONY HORSFALL

Metaphors for ministry

Just as a nursing mother cares for her children, so we cared for you. Because we loved you so much, we were delighted to share with you not only the gospel of God but our lives as well… For you know that we dealt with each of you as a father deals with his own children, encouraging, comforting and urging you to live lives worthy of God, who calls you into his kingdom and glory.

Paul is sometimes seen as a strong-minded pioneer, charging forward on his mission with little sensitivity towards people, but the section 2:1–16 sheds a different light on his manner and approach. Here are two metaphors for ministry to characterise his relationship with the Thessalonians, providing also an example for Christian ministry today.

First, Paul compares himself to a nursing mother, who, in love and gentleness, looks after her young children. For Paul, this meant not only sharing a message of words but also getting involved personally in the lives of those he met. He had a deep, genuine love for the Thessalonians, which meant he worked hard, not only preaching and teaching but also earning his living (presumably by making tents, Acts 18:3), so as not to burden them financially. He shared his life with them, living before them in authenticity and vulnerability.

Second, he dealt with them as a loving father deals with his children. He set them a good example of holy living and encouraged them to do the same. His words and his life were in harmony, so his appeal to live in a way worthy of God carried weight and brought challenge.

In a world full of charlatans, it was always Paul's concern to make sure that he never operated in the same way as them. Instead, he saw himself as one entrusted by God with the gospel, discharging his responsibility as one approved by him and with complete integrity (1 Thessalonians 2:3–6).

Ask God to help you care for others with the gentle love of a 'nursing mother' (v. 7). When there is a need to urge others on to better things, pray that you may do so by your example and wise words, as would an affectionate father (vv. 11–12).

TONY HORSFALL

Called to suffering

And we also thank God continually because, when you received the word of God… you accepted it not as a human word, but as it actually is, the word of God, which is indeed at work in you who believe. For you, brothers and sisters, became imitators of God's churches in Judea, which are in Christ Jesus: you suffered from your own people the same things those churches suffered from the Jews who killed the Lord Jesus and the prophets and also drove us out.

The Thessalonian church was born into a context of suffering. Persecution was a reality from the start, as Jason and his friends knew full well (Acts 17:5–9), and it increased as the days went by. In this they were not unique, but simply experiencing what the churches in Judea had already gone through, following the pattern of Jesus.

Paul had himself been a persecutor of the church, responsible in his former life as a zealous Pharisee for imprisoning believers and seeking to stamp out the new movement called The Way (Galatians 1:13; 1 Timothy 1:13). After his conversion, he joined the ranks of the persecuted, suffering more than most. When inviting people to follow Jesus, he never shied away from warning them that following him could mean persecution and suffering. His message was clear: 'We must go through many hardships to enter the kingdom of God' (Acts 14:22). At Thessalonica, he had been equally honest: 'We kept telling you that we would be persecuted' (1 Thessalonians 3:4).

In many parts of the world today, Christians accept that they, too, will suffer for the privilege of knowing Jesus. They embrace this harsh fact of life as part of the reality of discipleship. Perhaps, like me, you have been deeply moved to hear of the atrocities committed against our fellow believers in Middle Eastern countries and elsewhere. Even in Britain, as Christianity is increasingly marginalised, we are beginning to realise that there is a cost to following Jesus and those who stand up for gospel values may well find themselves victimised for their beliefs. If persecution comes to us, are we ready to stand firm?

Lord, grant strength and grace to those who suffer for you.

TONY HORSFALL

Frustrated and concerned

But, brothers and sisters, when we were orphaned by being separated from you for a short time (in person, not in thought), out of our intense longing we made every effort to see you. For we wanted to come to you... but Satan blocked our way... So when we could stand it no longer... we sent Timothy... to strengthen and encourage you in your faith, so that no one would be unsettled by these trials.

The caring heart that Paul had developed for the Thessalonians meant that he felt bereft when he was separated from them. He was anxious lest they had given way under the pressures they were experiencing and allowed Satan to entice them into unbelief (3:5).

His absence was not a sign of neglect or lack of concern. He simply had not been able to return, despite his longing to do so. Paul's explanation for this is rather sketchy: 'but Satan blocked our way' (2:18). The word he uses suggests 'cutting up the path' so that he could not get back to them. Presumably this speaks of the obstacles and hindrances he experienced.

We should not overemphasise the work of Satan, but neither should we be naïve enough to think we are not at times involved in spiritual conflict. The enemy of souls is always trying to snatch away the word of God from those who would believe (Mark 4:15) and often frustrates our attempts to serve God. Sometimes we experience a series of practical disasters—accidents, things breaking down, plans going awry. We may be dogged by illness and minor ailments, relationship breakdowns or communication problems. Although Satan has many ways to hinder the work of God, we need not fear, because God remains in control.

Are you experiencing frustrations and hindrances today as you seek to serve God? It may be that Satan is actively opposing what God is doing in your life or, through you, the lives of others. Remember to wear the armour of God (Ephesians 6:10–18). Resist Satan in prayer (James 4:7) and consider whether God might have another way for you to accomplish your objectives.

Lord, help me to stand firm.

TONY HORSFALL

The call to holiness

It is God's will that you should be sanctified: that you should avoid sexual immorality; that each of you should learn to control your own body in a way that is holy and honourable, not in passionate lust like the pagans, who do not know God; and that... no one should wrong or take advantage of a brother or sister. The Lord will punish all those who commit such sins, as we told you and warned you before.

Paul's teaching in Thessalonica focused not only on suffering but also on the call to a holy life. Following Jesus would mean a different way of life from the one they had been living before, particularly in the realm of sexual ethics.

Christians are often accused of being prudish and, in a society where anything goes sexually, of being repressive and guilt-ridden. Paul here associates sexual purity not with a negative attitude towards sex, but with a positive desire to do the will of God.

The heart of Christian teaching about sex stems from the belief that the body is a temple of the Holy Spirit (1 Corinthians 6:18–20). Once we realise that God actually lives within our human body, we are inclined to treat it (and the bodies of others) with much greater respect. Sexual immorality—by which is meant promiscuous living—only damages the body, as is seen in the spread of sexually transmitted diseases among those who choose such a lifestyle.

Furthermore, to be at the mercy of uncontrolled sexual desires leads only to sexual addiction—an addiction as destructive and harmful as any other kind. If the gratification of sexual impulses is the only thing a person lives for, then it will have severe repercussions on all his or her relationships. Casual sex and casual relationships leave much pain, anger and brokenness in their wake, not to mention deep regret.

God's call to holiness is a call to self-respect, self-control and to honour our bodies. Spirituality is deeply rooted in the physical, and how we use (or misuse) our bodies says a lot about us. Sex is a beautiful gift from God, but it belongs within the safety of the marriage relationship.

Lord, may my life reflect the beauty of your holiness.

TONY HORSFALL

God in the ordinary

Now about your love for one another we do not need to write to you, for you yourselves have been taught by God to love each other... Yet we urge you, brothers and sisters, to do so more and more, and to make it your ambition to lead a quiet life: you should mind your own business and work with your hands... so that your daily life may win the respect of outsiders and so that you will not be dependent on anybody.

One thing I love about Christian spirituality is that it is down to earth. It has practical application. We live out our faith not just on Sundays but also during the whole week, and not just in the isolation of a Christian subculture but also in the rough and tumble of the working world.

Learning to love other people starts with our fellow believers. It has always seemed to me that God's idea for the church—that anyone can join, regardless of their personality, brokenness or idiosyncrasies—is a recipe for disaster. Sometimes it is, if people have not learned how to love one another. That is why Paul congratulates the Thessalonians on the progress they have made in loving one another, but, at the same time, he urges them (with God's help) to do so 'more and more' (v. 10). If we are to fulfil the new commandment to love one another (John 13:34–35), we can never have enough divine love in our hearts.

Discipleship is not restricted to church fellowship, however. It is expressed in how we conduct ourselves at work and as we rub shoulders with other people, most of whom will not be believers. The expression 'to lead a quiet life' (v. 11) is usually taken to mean a trouble-free exist-ence, but Paul has something deeper in mind. The word 'quiet' is sug-gestive of inner stillness and rest—perhaps a reference to a contemplative approach to life that forms the bedrock of daily living, which by its very calmness becomes attractive to others.

This is his recipe for a faith that counts: love others genuinely and quietly get on with your work.

Lord, make me more loving and more centred on you.

TONY HORSFALL

Believers who have died

Brothers and sisters, we do not want you to be uninformed about those who sleep in death, so that you do not grieve like the rest of mankind, who have no hope. For we believe that Jesus died and rose again, and so we believe that God will bring with Jesus those who have fallen asleep in him. According to the Lord's word, we tell you that we who are still alive, who are left until the coming of the Lord, will certainly not precede those who have fallen asleep.

Paul taught that Jesus would return again and that believers should live in readiness for his appearing. This, however, created a question in the minds of some. What had happened to those who had died already and how would the return of Jesus affect them?

Even for people of faith, the death of a loved one is a sad and painful separation, but how much more so must it be for those who have no confidence in an afterlife? Paul reassures the Thessalonians by reminding them of the Christian hope that, for the believer, dying is like falling asleep and waking in the presence of Jesus. Yes, it is a sad separation, sometimes tragically so and particularly for those left behind, but it is not the end and, for the person who dies, it is the beginning of a whole new existence.

Furthermore, Christians have the assurance that when Jesus returns, he will bring with him those believers who have already died. They will form part of his glorious retinue, along with the angelic hosts, so they will not miss out on his coming either. They will be as involved as those who are alive at that momentous moment.

The word used for 'coming' in Greek is *parousia*, often used as a technical term referring to the visit of a king or emperor to a province under their rule. It reminds us that, one day, there will be a personal, powerful visitation by Jesus the king. When he comes again, it will not be in weakness but in power, heralding the reuniting of all his people—those alive and those who have died. Such is the hope we have.

Lord, thank you for such an assurance and hope.

TONY HORSFALL

The return of Jesus

For the Lord himself will come down from heaven, with a loud command, with the voice of the archangel and with the trumpet call of God, and the dead in Christ will rise first. After that, we who are still alive and are left will be caught up together with them in the clouds to meet the Lord in the air. And so we will be with the Lord for ever. Therefore encourage one another with these words.

Paul continues here to outline his understanding of what will happen when Jesus returns, by describing four important events.

First, the Lord himself will return. This will be the same Jesus who died and rose again, then ascended on high (Acts 1:11). This time his coming will not be to save but to rule, and he will be displayed not as the dying Saviour but as the reigning Lord. Then the dead in Christ will rise. They will receive new resurrection bodies just like the risen Christ (1 Corinthians 15:20–23).

Next, those who are alive will be caught up with them. Sometimes called 'the rapture', this dramatic event is often described in more detail than scripture warrants, but there will definitely be a supernatural event bringing Christ and his people together again (1 Corinthians 15:50–53). Finally, we will be with the Lord for ever. There will be no more separation, either between believers alive or dead or between Christ in heaven and his church on earth. This momentous event will usher in the coming of the kingdom on earth and the judgement of the wicked.

There is much that Paul does not say here about future events, but he says enough to give us a strong basis for mutual encouragement, and that is the main point of his teaching. We are not to fascinate each other—or argue—over various interpretations of events and the order of their occurrence. Rather, we should encourage one another with the joyful expectation that our Lord will return in glory and we shall be together, with him, for ever.

Many thoughts about future events are best held lightly. In time, all will be revealed; for now, we rejoice in the certainty of Christ's return.

Lord, we wait expectantly for your return.

TONY HORSFALL

Prayerful advice

Rejoice always, pray continually, give thanks in all circumstances; for this is God's will for you in Christ Jesus. Do not quench the Spirit. Do not treat prophecies with contempt but test them all; hold on to what is good, reject every kind of evil. May God himself, the God of peace, sanctify you through and through. May your whole spirit, soul and body be kept blameless at the coming of our Lord Jesus Christ. The one who calls you is faithful, and he will do it.

This concentrated piece of apostolic wisdom pours out of Paul's heart as he thinks of the Thessalonian church. He is eager to give the believers advice that will help them stand firm in their trials, yet is as concise as possible. Almost imperceptibly, his exhortation turns into prayer. If there is one thing he can do for this fledgling church at such a delicate time, it is to intercede on their behalf.

Both letters to Thessalonica are saturated with prayer. Indeed, no other epistles are so characterised by prayer. It feels as if prayer is the very air the apostle breathes, and he moves in and out of it even as he is writing. Prayer forms the backdrop for his relationship with them, his thankful heart glorifying God for his work among them (1 Thessalonians 1:2–3; 2 Thessalonians 1:3). At certain moments, prayers shoot heavenwards like arrows (1 Thessalonians 3:11; 2 Thessalonians 3:5, 16), each expressing his deep-seated desires for their well-being.

Some of his prayers, however, are more consciously formulated, like the one in today's passage, in which he asks that the work of God will run deeply within them to touch every fibre of their being. Elsewhere, he prays specifically that God will increase their love for one another and strengthen their faith (1 Thessalonians 3:12–13), that God's power will enable them to fulfil his purpose for them (2 Thessalonians 1:11–12) and that they will be encouraged by God (2 Thessalonians 2:16).

We can learn much from the apostle about how to pray for one another. Why not make these prayers your own, taking the apostle's words and using them as the basis for your own intercessions?

Lord, teach me to pray effectively.

TONY HORSFALL

The coming of Jesus

> God is just: he will pay back trouble to those who trouble you and give relief to you who are troubled, and to us as well. This will happen when the Lord Jesus is revealed from heaven in blazing fire with his powerful angels. He will punish those who do not know God and do not obey the gospel of our Lord Jesus. They will be punished with everlasting destruction and shut out from the presence of the Lord and from the glory of his might.

Paul's second letter to Thessalonica immediately picks up the theme of the second coming, showing its centrality to his message. His earlier teaching focused on what the return of the king would mean for the church, but here he explains it in the light of God's justice.

A moral universe requires some form of accountability. Evil must be punished, otherwise why do what is good? The world often appears full of injustice, with evildoers going unpunished. There is a universal cry for justice that includes the people of God as well. As in Thessalonica then, the church worldwide today is increasingly persecuted and its members opposed, ridiculed, imprisoned, tortured and killed. We may rightly ask, 'Why does God allow evil to triumph?'

The answer is that there will be a day of accountability, which will take place when Jesus returns as judge. His coming will be like an unveiling and he will be seen in the splendour of his holiness—not as a vulnerable baby in a manger, but as the ruling Lord and judge.

Those who have deliberately set themselves to oppose God, who have persistently rejected the offer of salvation and instead sought to thwart his purposes on earth, will be excluded from the presence of God for ever—shut off from the light, trapped in the darkness they have chosen for themselves.

Those, however, who have believed will share his presence. They will marvel when his glory is revealed and their suffering will seem as nothing as they delight in his presence and their vindication. No wonder the cry of God's people is 'Amen. Come, Lord Jesus' (Revelation 22:20).

Lord, hear our cry. Let your kingdom come.

TONY HORSFALL

Things to come (part 1)

Concerning the coming of our Lord Jesus Christ and our being gathered to him, we ask you, brothers and sisters, not to become easily unsettled or alarmed by the teaching allegedly from us—whether by a prophecy or by word of mouth or by letter—asserting that the day of the Lord has already come. Don't let anyone deceive you in any way, for that day will not come until the rebellion occurs and the man of lawlessness is revealed, the man doomed to destruction.

No other Christian doctrine has attracted so much unhelpful speculation as that of the second coming and surrounding events. Indeed, many people prefer to avoid teaching about Jesus' return rather than get embroiled in competing interpretations. Yet Paul writes about it in detail and we cannot ignore his teaching.

In Thessalonica, within a short period after Paul had left, false teachers were claiming (supposedly with his authorisation) that the day of the Lord had already taken place. He dismisses their claims, reminding the Thessalonians that two things must happen before Jesus returns: a 'rebellion' and the coming of 'the man of lawlessness' (v. 3). Paul had spoken in depth about these events (2:5), but the Thessalonians had forgotten his teaching. Part of our difficulty is that we do not know all that he previously taught, so it is hard to understand everything he says here.

'The man of lawlessness', often called the Antichrist, has been variously identified down the centuries, but, as he has not yet appeared, we cannot know his true identity. It is clear, though, that he will be a real person, completely opposed to the law of God, who encourages others into increasingly lawless behaviour. His appearance will release into the world a tsunami of wickedness (the 'rebellion'), when societies worldwide will see normal standards of behaviour overthrown and God's laws rejected. Other passages in Paul's writings warn of a terrible time that will herald the Lord's return (1 Timothy 4:1; 2 Timothy 3:1–5). Jesus, too, spoke of a time of increasing wickedness (Matthew 24:1–14).

How reassuring to know that God has the future under his control!

Lord, do not let evil triumph; reveal yourself in glory.

TONY HORSFALL

135

Things to come (part 2)

And now you know what is holding him back, so that he may be revealed at the proper time. For the secret power of lawlessness is already at work; but the one who now holds it back will continue to do so till he is taken out of the way. And then the lawless one will be revealed, whom the Lord Jesus will overthrow with the breath of his mouth and destroy by the splendour of his coming.

As Paul goes into detail about the events surrounding Jesus' return, we learn that even these happen at 'the proper time' (v. 6)—that is, according to God's timetable. The rise of evil and the appearance of the Antichrist are held in check until God allows things to change.

Bible scholars debate exactly how the Antichrist is restrained, but the most likely interpretation is that the rule of law and the power of good government hold him back. Paul elsewhere recognises the importance of stable government as instituted by God (Romans 13:1–5). He urges prayer for those in authority, so that we can live in peace and the gospel be freely proclaimed (1 Timothy 2:1–2). The church prospers when the rule of law is upheld and God's laws are respected. A time will come, though, when God will allow the breakdown of this kind of government and, in that context, the Antichrist, who has been active all along but in a hidden way, will break to the surface and the rebellion will begin.

It is not hard to see how easily this can happen. Today we see most of God's laws broken and rejected by a society pursuing its own godless agenda. Strident atheistic voices proclaim the irrelevance of God and his church. Moral absolutes are no more and sexual behaviour is confused. Money is a god and consumerism reigns. Children are abused and young girls trafficked for sex. Terrorism murderously straddles the globe. Surely the pace is gathering as we hurtle towards the events described by the apostle?

Yet, as believers, we do not fear because we know that the Lord will return and defeat the powers of darkness. This is our hope in difficult times.

Lord, keep us at peace in the knowledge of your ultimate victory.

TONY HORSFALL

Stand firm! Hold fast!

So then, brothers and sisters, stand firm and hold fast to the teachings
we passed on to you, whether by word of mouth or by letter. May our
Lord Jesus Christ himself and God our Father, who loved us and by his
grace gave us eternal encouragement and good hope, encourage your
hearts and strengthen you in every good deed and word.

Paul feared that the Thessalonians might be unsettled in their faith by
the trials they were experiencing and the difficulties with the false teachers. He wrote this letter to reassure and remind them of his teachings
so that this would not happen. He has a double exhortation for them in
the current situation: stand firm (resting on what you were taught) and
hold fast (to that which you believed in the beginning).

Christian stability is crucial in times of change and uncertainty. When
evil abounds and various winds of doctrine are blowing, it is easy to be
tossed about emotionally and spiritually (Ephesians 4:14). At such
times, it is imperative that we ground ourselves in the unchanging truths
of God's word. This means focusing on study, meditation and prayer so
that we know the truth for ourselves and are not easily deceived.

At the same time, Paul offers a prayer for them, asking God to
strengthen and encourage them so that their service on his behalf may
continue without interruption. Paul rejoices that God has begun a good
work in them (2 Thessalonians 1:1–4; 2:13–14) and asks this same
faithful God to continue his work.

Paul's prayer is based on two things he knows about God with abso-
lute certainty. First, he is a God of love who has set his love on them (v.
13; 1 Thessalonians 1:4). It is this love that caused God to reach out and
take hold of them in the first place, and such unchanging love means he
will not abandon them now. Second, he is a God of grace who has gifted
them already with encouragement and hope. How could such a generous God suddenly skimp in his blessing towards his children?

No, they are safe because they are God's—and so are we.

Lord, help me to stand firm in you and hold tightly to your truth.

TONY HORSFALL

Supporting BRF
with a gift in your will

Throughout its history, BRF's ministry has been enabled thanks to the generosity of those who have shared its vision and supported its work both by giving during their lifetime and also through legacy gifts.

BRF is a charity that is passionate about making a difference through the Christian faith. We want to see lives and communities transformed through our creative programmes and resources for individuals, churches and schools. We are doing this by resourcing:

- Christian growth and understanding of the Bible by people of all ages through our Bible reading notes, other published resources and events.
- Churches for outreach in the local community through Messy Church, Who Let The Dads Out? and The Gift of Years.
- The teaching of Christianity within primary schools through our Barnabas in Schools programme.
- Children's and family ministry in churches through our websites and published resources.

Legacies make a significant difference to our ability to achieve our purpose. A legacy gift would help fund the development and sustainability of BRF's work into the future. We hope you may consider a gift to help us continue to take this work forward in the decades to come.

For further information about making a gift to BRF in your will or to discuss how a specific bequest could be used to develop our ministry, please contact Sophie Aldred (Head of Fundraising) or Richard Fisher (Chief Executive) by email at fundraising@brf.org. uk or by phone on 01865 319700.

The BRF

Magazine

Journey through Lent

Kristina Petersen

'I hope you like shortbread,' said my friend. 'I do, but I've given it up for Lent,' was my reply. 'Oh no! I thought you'd only given up chocolate. I bought the shortbread especially for you!' With this, I discovered one of the pitfalls of giving up sweet treats for Lent.

What is the point of Lent? Surely there is more to it than giving up sweets, chocolate, alcohol or Facebook, or even taking up some kind of good habit or reading a Lent book? According to the Oxford English Dictionary, Lent is 'the period preceding Easter, which is devoted to fasting, abstinence, and penitence in commemoration of Christ's fasting in the wilderness. In the Western Church it runs from Ash Wednesday to Holy Saturday, and so includes 40 weekdays.'

What would be true fasting for us—fasting that strips us of the external methods that we use to distract ourselves, which ultimately keep us away from God? Jesus was full of the Holy Spirit and was led by that very same Spirit into the desert, where he was tempted (Luke 4:1–2; see verses 1–13 for the full story). After being affirmed by God and before starting his ministry, he needed to experience a desert time, a time to think about his ministry and his priorities. Stripped of all support systems, hungry and possibly lonely, he was tempted to use some short cuts to reach his aims: after all, what would be wrong with using authority and splendour to reach the world? Surely, throwing himself from the highest point of the temple and allowing angels to rescue him would demonstrate the power of God to those visiting the temple? Jesus, however, not only knew the scriptures but was also listening to his Father and knew his Father's will for him, which did not include doing miracles for their own sake.

What are our temptations when all our support systems are stripped from us? What do we do when things go wrong? Do you reach for the chocolate, a glass of wine, your mobile phone, the computer keyboard or the remote control when you need comfort after a bad day? We all have ways of distracting ourselves and of numbing pain after a difficult experience. This is not wrong in itself but it can prevent us from facing issues and dealing with the source of pain, and it can stop us from turning to God. Why is he not our first port of call when things go wrong?

Jesus is led into the desert because he needs this time before starting his public ministry, before he teaches and heals, before he faces rejection and ridicule. It is a training ground, a necessary preparation for his ministry. What do we need in order to be able to give out and minister to others? Sometimes we need to be forced to come face to face with ourselves and with God. Going on a retreat (without our mobile phones) can do that, but so can going to live as part of a community, working with others for a common goal, or spending time immersed in a different culture. Alternatively, we can simply remove some of our external securities—whatever it is that we use to distract ourselves (TV, books, food, the internet). Who are you when all these things are stripped away? What do you need to give up to become more truly yourself, and to come closer to God?

In fact, what image of God do we have? This may also be something to give up. 'If we're to draw closer to God, we need to be willing to give up some of our entrenched ideas about God in order to see him more clearly... We need to allow the light to be shed on those places where our idea of God is too harsh, too weak, too small, too fragile, too stern (Maggi Dawn, *Giving It Up*, BRF, 2009). Being removed from external distractions can bring us face to face not only with ourselves but also with our image of God. It can enable us to hear more clearly from him, and, when he speaks to us, we may be in for a surprise!

Once we have journeyed through the desert, we are better equipped to reach out to others. 'Is not this the kind of fasting I have chosen: to loose the chains of injustice and untie the cords of the yoke, to set the oppressed free and break every yoke?' (Isaiah 58:6, NIV). If Lent is a time when we focus only on ourselves, it could be quite self-indulgent. Jesus went to Nazareth straight after his time in the desert. There, people rejected him and tried to stone him. Not an easy start to his public ministry! Yet he had been affirmed by his Father and had dealt with some temptations, and he was now ready to speak the truth, regardless of the reaction it would provoke.

What kind of fast does God require of us? What do you need to give up in order to hear him speak to you? What do you then need to take up in order to serve him? Lent can be a time of drawing closer to God, to our true selves and to other people. It can be a journey from the death of old habits to a new way of looking at life.

Oh, and I'll have a piece of that shortbread now, please.

Kristina Petersen is BRF's Editorial Coordinator. She lives in Oxford and is an accomplished linguist, fluent in German, English and Dutch.

Encountering the Risen Christ

Mark Bradford

For a while now, it has struck me as unusual how the church frequently misses the vital importance of Easter. Having been part of a church community all of my life, I remember the 'light-bulb' moment in my late teens when I came to realise that Christmas was not the main event in the church's calendar. I could never have guessed it from mere observation!

As Tom Wright has remarked, 'Take Christmas away, and in biblical terms you lose two chapters at the front of Matthew and Luke, nothing else. Take Easter away, and you don't have a New Testament; you don't have a Christianity' (*Surprised by Hope*, SPCK, 2007, pp. 256–57). So, no resurrection, no Christianity. If nothing really did happen that first Easter, then we pack up and go home. But if something did happen at Easter, then it changes everything.

Of course, this is what the church has always believed. The first apostles saw themselves as witnesses to the resurrection of Jesus. The heart of their message was to teach and proclaim that in Jesus there is resurrection from the dead (Romans 1:4). Sunday, being the day of resurrection, quickly became the day on which Christians gathered to worship the risen Christ together, and, from as early as the second century, the celebration of Easter took place as a season rather than merely a day. This season 'was regarded as a time of rejoicing, and every day was treated in the same way as Sunday—that is, with no kneeling for prayer or fasting' (Paul Bradshaw, *Early Christian Worship*, SPCK, 2010, p. 93).

Yet, in my experience, the contemporary church has lost a vital sense of the importance of Easter. Lent is often kept, with plenty of resources available for this 40-day period that prepares us for Easter, but, inexplicably, we celebrate Easter for only a single day. In the church calendar, Easter is not just a single day; it is a whole season. While Lent is 40 days long, the Easter season is 50. The energy put into our self-denial during Lent should be far outstripped, both in intensity and longevity, by the energy put into feasting and celebration during Easter.

My book, *Encountering the Risen Christ*, emerged out of a course I ran in my own church as a way of encouraging people to mark the Easter season far more intentionally. Over the seven-week period leading to Pentecost, we looked at the encounters that Mary, Thomas, Peter, Cleopas and his companion, and the disciples as a group had with the risen Christ. These encounters are some of the most intimate, striking and transformative stories to be found in the whole of the Bible.

There is a profound difference between a meeting and an encounter.

- Meetings are usually planned and predictable events. Encounters are often unplanned and can have consequences far beyond anything that we can imagine.
- Meetings tend to be fairly superficial affairs in which the 'usual business' is discussed. Encounters are deep affairs in which the agenda is not set by us.
- We can often walk out of meetings largely unaffected by what has happened. We will never leave an encounter unchanged. In fact, we may never to be the same again.

This was certainly the case for Mary, for the disciples, for Thomas, for Cleopas and his companion, and for Peter—as I explore in the book. In each of these stories, we find that the risen Christ shows up in the most ordinary of places and encounters the most ordinary of people, in order to lead them out of dead-end situations of brokenness and into new possibilities for life and healing and hope. And all because of what happened that first Easter Sunday.

Mary would journey with the risen Christ from sadness to hope; the disciples, from fear to confidence; Thomas, from doubt to confirmation; Cleopas and his companion, from shattered dreams to new beginnings; and Peter, from failure to restoration.

In the forthcoming season of Easter—between Easter Day and Pentecost—we are invited not only to listen in to these encounters but also to participate in them ourselves. We, too, have sadness, fear, doubts, shattered dreams and a sense of failure. The risen Christ invites us to journey with him toward fresh possibilities of hope, confidence, confirmation, new beginnings and restoration, because, if something did happen that first Easter, it offers the potential to change everything.

Mark Bradford is the author of Encountering the Risen Christ, *a book for the Easter season. It focuses on the main characters in the post-resurrection accounts, exploring how meeting the risen Christ transforms their lives. To order a copy, please turn to page 155.*

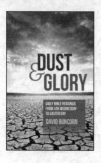

An extract from
Dust and Glory

Dust and Glory, BRF's Lent book for 2016, has been written to accompany you through this special period of prayer and self-examination, a time of turning from winter to spring, from death to life. In this book, the questions are as important as the answers, and may call us to deep heart-searching. Author David Runcorn's goal is to draw us to authentic faith that acknowledges both the dust of our mortality and the glory that keeps breaking in with unexpected life, hope and new beginnings. The following extract, 'Holy laughter', is for the Fourth Sunday of Lent.

As the first day of the week was dawning, Mary Magdalene and the other Mary went to see the tomb. And suddenly there was a great earthquake; for an angel of the Lord, descending from heaven, came and rolled back the stone and sat on it... The angel said to the women, 'Do not be afraid; I know that you are looking for Jesus who was cruci-fied. He is not here; for he has been raised, as he said. Come, see the place where he lay. Then go quickly and tell his disciples, "He has been raised from the dead."'... So they left the tomb quickly with fear and great joy, and ran to tell his disciples.

MATTHEW 28:1–2, 5–8 (NRSV)

Stories told too often can easily lose their capacity to surprise. We know them too well. So, when approaching the major seasons of the Christian faith, I pray for one insight or thought to come fresh to me. Last Easter it came in this story, with the angel who 'rolled back the stone and sat on it'—that detail. I can imagine that rolling a heavy stone away on your own would leave you out of breath but I never considered it might be a problem for angels.

Sitting down has a 'job done' feel to it. It is the way we picture Jesus at the right hand of God. Certainly, while the angel is sitting on it, there is no chance that anyone could roll the stone back again. The mood feels teasingly casual, somehow. Something solid enough to seal in death itself is reduced to a handy spot to sit for a moment.

We surely do not suppose that the stone was rolled away to let Jesus out. If death could not hold him, a stone would be no obstacle. Rather, it was rolled away to let us in. There is a discovery for us to make. I fancy the angel fixing me with a mischievous 'You won't believe what I've just seen!' smile. Actually, this morning I think he winked at me! I am trying to pray but I keep giggling.

There is a literary theory that all storytelling revolves around four types of plot, which correspond to the seasons of creation: autumn is tragedy, winter is satire, summer is romance and spring is comedy. Resurrection is a sign of spring-time. New life is emerging after the long death of winter, and this is the season of comedy.

It may be that our most trusting response to the resurrection story is laughter. Let the lawyers and theologians do the serious analysis, but do not miss the angel sitting on that stone watching us all, grinning. How did the angels in the tomb contain themselves, waiting for the first bewildered witnesses. 'Shh, they're coming!' Well, wouldn't you, on a day like that?

> *It may be that our most trusting response to the resurrection story is laughter*

The poet Anne Sexton was often left bruised in her pilgrimage through faith and life, but in one of her most moving poems she imagines meeting up with God, who surprises her by producing a pack of cards and playing poker with her. She is dealt a hand, as, in a sense, we all are in this life. We make what we can of what we find in our grasp. To her surprise, it is a very strong hand. She thinks she has won. Then God trumps her with a fifth ace! He cheats—he breaks the rules—but her response is not outrage. She loves it! The poem ends with the poet and God doubled over each other in helpless laughter at their 'double triumphs' ('The rowing endeth' in *The Complete Poems*, Houghton Mifflin, 1982, pp. 473–74).

I once invited a prayer group to silently imagine they were entering the court of God the king. They were to draw near with whatever expressions of reverence they felt appropriate. The mood was serious until someone suddenly laughed out loud. I asked afterwards what had happened. 'Well, you know when you are in the presence of someone really important, you feel awkward and tongue-tied and they say something to relax you?'

'Yes,' I said.'

'Well, God told me a joke.'

There is an important tradition, in many older societies, of the clown or jester. In royal courts, among religious dignitaries and in the marketplaces, they have permission to mock the pomposity of the powerful and dethrone the self-important. They laugh at the po-faced solemnity that we confuse with reverence. They simply refuse to take us seriously—and that is their gift. Their laughter relativises the powers. They roll large and important stones away and just sit on them.

This is the season of comedy. Resurrection is God's fifth ace. He has broken the rules. You just have to laugh, don't you?

Prayer: Lord, teach me to trust enough to laugh.

David Runcorn is a popular writer, speaker, teacher, retreat leader and spiritual guide. His books include The Spirituality Workbook: a guide for pilgrims, explorers and seekers *and* Fear and Trust: God-centred leadership. *He lives in Gloucester, where he is involved with the selection, training and support of people called to Christian ministry of all kinds.*

To order a copy of this book, please turn to page 155. Alternatively, it is available at Christian bookshops.

Recommended reading

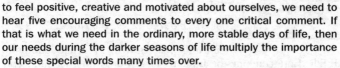

Kevin Ball

Encouragement and hope—two words that can brighten even the darkest of days. It is said that, to feel positive, creative and motivated about ourselves, we need to hear five encouraging comments to every one critical comment. If that is what we need in the ordinary, more stable days of life, then our needs during the darker seasons of life multiply the importance of these special words many times over.

The best way to encourage someone, of course, is to be right there alongside them in person, but the busy, demanding aspects of life often make this impossible. It's in these cases that an encouraging gift may be just what is needed. January 2016 sees the publication of two new gift books of encouragement and hope.

The Recovery of Hope
Bible reflections for sensing God's presence and hearing God's call
Naomi Starkey

pb, 978 0 85746 417 0, 144 pages, £8.99

Naomi Starkey, editor of *New Daylight* for the last 15 years, has brought together, in her new book *The Recovery of Hope*, a selection of her own *New Daylight* readings covering these themes, along with some newly written poems of reflection.

Naomi writes, 'As I reviewed my contributions to *New Daylight*, I found that I have been drawn to a recognisable pattern of themes that related to my pilgrimage of faith: the hunger for God's consoling presence especially during hard times, the challenge to respond to his call on my life, and the discovery—and rediscovery, again and again—of the deep reassurance that I am not only known but loved beyond understanding.

'So I have woven these Bible readings into a kind of journey towards the recovery of hope, the hope of experiencing first-hand the utter sufficiency of God's grace, love and forgiveness, a hope that we may know with our heads for a while—perhaps even a long while—before we truly feel it in our hearts. It is the hope of knowing God not only as consoling presence in the darkness but in the challenge of responding to his call and in the transformative experience of knowing how much we are his beloved children.'

Postcards from Heaven
Words and pictures to help you hear from God
Ellie Hart
pb, 978 0 85746 427 9, 160 pages, £7.99

Postcards from Heaven, by a new author to BRF, Ellie Hart, combines beautiful pastel artwork with brief but deeply touching reflections of encouragement and hope on the seasons of life.

Ellie writes, 'We all live in a season of one kind or another, a season of work, a season of ministry, a season of looking after children, a season of joy, a season of grieving, seasons of friendship and relationships. The main feature of seasons is that they don't last forever: the place we move into next will be different in many ways.

'Last summer, a friend of mine who hears God more clearly, perhaps, than anyone else I know came and told me that the Father wanted me to write a book about the seasons that we go through in life, especially about how to get through the tougher seasons and how to navigate those curious empty spaces that come in between seasons of activity.

'So I've done my best, and my heart's desire is that this book could become a place where you encounter our wonderful, beautiful, untameable, passionate, loving God and hear him speak directly to you in whatever circumstance you find yourself in.'

Immeasurably more…

Every time I stand on the beach I scoop up as much water as I can hold in my hands and I think, 'This is how much of God's presence, power and peace I have experienced so far.' Then I look out at the sea. The difference between the water I can hold in my hands and the contents of the Mediterranean Sea (and then the Atlantic Ocean) is beyond my ability to comprehend. That's how much more there is to explore of God; that's how much more he has for you. You just need to ask (page 69).

A Christian Guide to Environmental Issues
Martin J. Hodson and Margot R. Hodson
pb, 978 0 85746 383 8, 224 pages £9.99

Encouragement and hope are two qualities that husband and wife authors Margot and Martin Hodson are anxious to find in the deeply concerning issues relating to planet earth's environment and its ongoing ability to support life.

A Christian Guide to Environmental Issues explains the issues, not focusing just on global warming but also examining:

- biodiversity and the loss of many animal species because of the activities of humans—a process now being termed the sixth great extinction event.
- the pressure on clean water supplies. This is best illustrated by the fact that the amount of fresh water available today is pretty much as it was 2000 years ago, but today the world's population is 7 billion and still growing—not the 250 million of the time of Jesus.
- the provision of energy to supply businesses and homes, the impact of fossil fuels on the environment and the slow development of and opposition to alternative energy systems.
- the continued focus by governments on economic growth driven by increased consumption, seeming to ignore the fact that the world's natural resources are limited. If the world's precious natural resources were shared sustainably and equally among its population today, we would all need to adopt the lifestyle of a country such as the Sudan.

What can we actually do? Environmental experts Margot and Martin not only lead you through the facts and figures but help you to explore the issues from a biblical point of view, showing the importance of the creation in God's redemptive plan and our responsibility in its management.

This book is ideal for church groups or individuals wanting to explore the issues intelligently and get involved. Communities will need to come together, understand the realities, accept the lifestyle changes required and then effectively lobby to encourage political leaders to prioritise the issues, so that a much-needed hope can be realised.

To find out more, to read sample chapters and to order online, visit www. brfonline.org.uk. Alternatively you can order using the form on page 155.

SUPPORTING BRF'S MINISTRY

As a Christian charity, BRF is involved in eight complementary areas.

- **BRF** (www.brf.org.uk) resources adults for their spiritual journey through Bible reading notes, books and Quiet Days. BRF also provides the infrastructure that supports our other specialist ministries.
- **Foundations21** (www.foundations21.net) provides flexible and innovative ways for individuals and groups to explore their Christian faith and discipleship through a multimedia internet-based resource.
- **Messy Church** (www.messychurch.org.uk), led by Lucy Moore, enables churches all over the UK (and increasingly abroad) to reach children and adults beyond the fringes of the church.
- **Barnabas in Churches** (www.barnabasinchurches.org.uk) helps churches to support, resource and develop their children's ministry with the under-11s more effectively .
- **Barnabas in Schools** (www.barnabasinschools.org.uk) enables primary school children and teachers to explore Christianity creatively and bring the Bible alive within RE and Collective Worship.
- **Faith in Homes** (www.faithinhomes.org.uk) supports families to explore and live out the Christian faith at home.
- **Who Let The Dads Out** (www.wholetthedadsout.org) inspires churches to engage with dads and their pre-school children.
- **The Gift of Years** (www.brf.org.uk/thegiftofyears) celebrates the blessings of long life and seeks to meet the spiritual needs of older people.

At the heart of BRF's ministry is a desire to equip adults and children for Christian living—helping them to read and understand the Bible, explore prayer and grow as disciples of Jesus. We need your help to make an impact on the local church, local schools and the wider community.

- You could support BRF's ministry with a one-off gift or regular donation (using the response form on page 153).
- You could consider making a bequest to BRF in your will.
- You could encourage your church to support BRF as part of your church's giving to home mission—perhaps focusing on a specific area of our ministry, or a particular member of our Barnabas team.
- Most important of all, you could support BRF with your prayers.

If you would like to discuss how a specific gift or bequest could be used in the development of our ministry, please phone 01865 319700 or email enquiries@brf.org.uk.

Whatever you can do or give, we thank you for your support.

BRF has been helping individuals connect with the Bible for over 90 years. We want to support churches as they seek to encourage church members into regular Bible reading.

Order a Bible reading resources pack

This pack is designed to give your church the tools to publicise our Bible reading notes. It includes:

- Sample Bible reading notes for your congregation to try.
- Publicity resources, including a poster.
- A church magazine feature about Bible reading notes.

The pack is free, but we welcome a £5 donation to cover the cost of postage. If you require a pack to be sent outside the UK or require a specific number of sample Bible reading notes, please contact us for postage costs. More information about what the current pack contains is available on our website.

How to order and find out more

- Visit **www.biblereadingnotes.org.uk/for-churches/**
- Telephone BRF on 01865 319700 between 9.15 am and 5.30 pm.
- Write to us at BRF, 15 The Chambers, Vineyard, Abingdon, OX14 3FE

Keep informed about our latest initiatives

We are continuing to develop resources to help churches encourage people into regular Bible reading, wherever they are on their journey. Join our email list at **www.biblereadingnotes.org.uk/helpingchurches/** to stay informed about the latest initiatives that your church could benefit from.

Introduce a friend to our notes

We can send information about our notes and current prices for you to pass on. Please contact us.

Please note our subscription rates 2016–2017. From the May 2016 issue, the new subscription rates will be:

Individual subscriptions covering 3 issues for under 5 copies, payable in advance (including postage and packing):

	UK	Eur/Economy	Airmail
NEW DAYLIGHT each set of 3 p.a.	£16.35	£24.90	£28.20
NEW DAYLIGHT 3-year sub (i.e. 9 issues) (Not available for Deluxe)	£43.20	N/A	N/A
NEW DAYLIGHT DELUXE each set of 3 p.a.	£20.70	£33.75	£40.50

Group subscriptions covering 3 issues for 5 copies or more, sent to ONE UK address (post free).

NEW DAYLIGHT	£13.05	each set of 3 p.a.
NEW DAYLIGHT DELUXE	£16.80	each set of 3 p.a.

Overseas group subscription rates available on request.
Contact enquiries@brf.org.uk.

Please note that the annual billing period for Group Subscriptions runs from 1 May to 30 April.

Copies of the notes may also be obtained from Christian bookshops:

NEW DAYLIGHT	£4.35 each copy
NEW DAYLIGHT DELUXE	£5.60 each copy

Visit www.biblereadingnotes.org.uk for information about our other Bible reading notes and Apple apps for iPhone and iPod touch.

BRF MINISTRY APPEAL RESPONSE FORM

I would like to help BRF. Please use my gift for:
☐ Where most needed ☐ Barnabas Children's Ministry ☐ Messy Church
☐ Who Let The Dads Out? ☐ The Gift of Years

Please complete all relevant sections of this form and print clearly.

Title _____ First name/initials _____ Surname _____

Address _____

_____ Postcode _____

Telephone _____ Email _____

Regular giving

If you would like to give by direct debit, please tick the box below and fill in details:

☐ I would like to make a regular gift of £ _____ per month / quarter / year
(delete as appropriate) by Direct Debit. (Please complete the form on page 159.)

If you would like to give by standing order, please contact Priscilla Kew (tel: 01235 462305; email priscilla.kew@brf.org.uk; write to BRF address below).

One-off donation

Please accept my special gift of
☐ £10 ☐ £50 ☐ £100 (other) £ _____ by

☐ Cheque / Charity Voucher payable to 'BRF'
☐ Visa / Mastercard / Charity Card
(delete as appropriate)

Name on card _____

Card no. [ ][ ][ ][ ] [ ][ ][ ][ ] [ ][ ][ ][ ] [ ][ ][ ][ ]

Start date [ ][ ] Expiry date [ ][ ][ ]

Security code [ ][ ]

Signature _____ Date _____

☐ I would like to give a legacy to BRF. Please send me further information.

☐ I want BRF to claim back tax on this gift.
(If you tick this box, please fill in gift aid declaration overleaf.)

Please detach and send this completed form to: BRF, 15 The Chambers, Vineyard, Abingdon OX14 3FE.

BRF is a Registered Charity (No.233280)

153

GIFT AID DECLARATION

Bible Reading Fellowship

Please treat as Gift Aid donations all qualifying gifts of money made:

today ☐   in the past 4 years ☐   in the future ☐

I confirm I have paid or will pay an amount of Income Tax and/or Capital Gains Tax for each tax year (6 April to 5 April) that is at least equal to the amount of tax that all the charities that I donate to will reclaim on my gifts for that tax year. I understand that other taxes such as VAT or Council Tax do not qualify. I understand that BRF will reclaim 25p of tax on every £1 that I give.

☐   My donation does not qualify for Gift Aid.

Signature _____

Date _____

Notes:

1. Please notify BRF if you want to cancel this declaration, change your name or home address, or no longer pay sufficient tax on your income and/or capital gains.

2. If you pay Income Tax at the higher/additional rate and want to receive the additional tax relief due to you, you must include all your Gift Aid donations on your Self-Assessment tax return or ask HM Revenue and Customs to adjust your tax code.

ND0116

BRF PUBLICATIONS ORDER FORM

Please send me the following book(s):

		Quantity	Price	Total
428 6	Encountering the Risen Christ (M. Bradford)	_____	£7.99	_____
357 9	Dust and Glory (D. Runcorn)	_____	£7.99	_____
417 0	The Recovery of Hope (N. Starkey)	_____	£7.99	_____
427 9	Postcards from Heaven (E. Hart)	_____	£7.99	_____
383 8	Christian Guide Environmental (M.&M. Hodson)	_____	£9.99	_____
680 1	Giving It Up (M. Dawn)	_____	£7.99	_____
	Quiet Spaces sample copy	_____	FREE	_____

Total cost of books £ _____
Donation £ _____
Postage and packing £ _____
TOTAL £ _____

POSTAGE AND PACKING CHARGES				
Order value	UK	Europe	Economy (Surface)	Standard (Air)
Under £7.00	£1.25	£3.00	£3.50	£5.50
£7.00–£29.99	£2.25	£5.50	£6.50	£10.00
£30.00 and over	free	prices on request		

Please complete the payment details below and send with payment to: **BRF, 15 The Chambers, Vineyard, Abingdon OX14 3FE**

Name _____

Address _____

_____ Postcode _____

Tel _____ Email _____

Total enclosed £ _____ (cheques should be made payable to 'BRF')

Please charge my Visa ❑ Mastercard ❑ Switch card ❑ with £ _____

Card no: ⬜⬜⬜⬜⬜⬜⬜⬜⬜⬜⬜⬜⬜⬜⬜⬜⬜⬜⬜⬜

Expires ⬜⬜⬜⬜ Security code ⬜⬜⬜

Issue no (Switch only) ⬜⬜⬜⬜

Signature (essential if paying by credit/Switch) _____

NEW DAYLIGHT INDIVIDUAL SUBSCRIPTIONS

❏ I would like to take out a subscription myself:

Your name _____

Your address _____

_____ Postcode _____

Tel _____ Email _____

Please send *New Daylight* beginning with the May 2016 / September 2016 /
January 2017 issue: (delete as applicable)

(please tick box)	UK	Europe/Economy	Airmail
NEW DAYLIGHT	❏ £16.35	❏ £24.90	❏ £28.20
NEW DAYLIGHT 3-year sub	❏ £43.20		
NEW DAYLIGHT DELUXE	❏ £20.70	❏ £33.75	❏ £40.50
NEW DAYLIGHT daily email only	❏ £13.05 (UK and overseas)		

Please complete the payment details below and send with appropriate
payment to: **BRF, 15 The Chambers, Vineyard, Abingdon OX14 3FE**

Total enclosed £ _____ (cheques should be made payable to 'BRF')

Please charge my Visa ❏ Mastercard ❏ Switch card ❏ with £ _____

Card no: | | | | | | | | | | | | | | | | |

Expires | | | | | Security code | | | |

Issue no (Switch only) | | | |

Signature (essential if paying by card) _____

To set up a direct debit, please also complete the form on page 159 and send
it to BRF with this form.

BRF is a Registered Charity

ND0116

NEW DAYLIGHT GIFT SUBSCRIPTIONS

❏ I would like to give a gift subscription (please provide both names and addresses:

Your name _____

Your address _____

_____ Postcode _____

Tel _____ Email _____

Gift subscription name _____

Gift subscription address _____

_____ Postcode _____

Gift message (20 words max. or include your own gift card for the recipient)

_____

_____

Please send *New Daylight* beginning with the May 2016 / September 2016 / January 2017 issue: (delete as applicable)

(please tick box)	UK	Europe/Economy	Airmail
NEW DAYLIGHT	❏ £16.35	❏ £24.90	❏ £28.20
NEW DAYLIGHT 3-year sub	❏ £43.20		
NEW DAYLIGHT DELUXE	❏ £20.70	❏ £33.75	❏ £40.50
NEW DAYLIGHT daily email only	❏ £13.05 (UK and overseas)		

Please complete the payment details below and send with appropriate payment to: **BRF, 15 The Chambers, Vineyard, Abingdon OX14 3FE**

Total enclosed £ _____ (cheques should be made payable to 'BRF')

Please charge my Visa ❏ Mastercard ❏ Switch card ❏ with £ _____

Card no: ☐☐☐☐☐☐☐☐☐☐☐☐☐☐☐☐☐☐

Expires ☐☐☐☐ Security code ☐☐☐

Issue no (Switch only) ☐☐☐☐

Signature (essential if paying by card) _____

To set up a direct debit, please also complete the form on page 159 and send it to BRF with this form.

DIRECT DEBIT PAYMENTS

Now you can pay for your annual subscription to BRF notes using Direct Debit. You need only give your bank details once, and the payment is made automatically every year until you cancel it. If you would like to pay by Direct Debit, please use the form opposite, entering your BRF account number under 'Reference'.

You are fully covered by the Direct Debit Guarantee:

The Direct Debit Guarantee

- This Guarantee is offered by all banks and building societies that accept instructions to pay Direct Debits.
- If there are any changes to the amount, date or frequency of your Direct Debit, The Bible Reading Fellowship will notify you 10 working days in advance of your account being debited or as otherwise agreed. If you request The Bible Reading Fellowship to collect a payment, confirmation of the amount and date will be given to you at the time of the request.
- If an error is made in the payment of your Direct Debit, by The Bible Reading Fellowship or your bank or building society, you are entitled to a full and immediate refund of the amount paid from your bank or building society.
  - – If you receive a refund you are not entitled to, you must pay it back when The Bible Reading Fellowship asks you to.
- You can cancel a Direct Debit at any time by simply contacting your bank or building society. Written confirmation may be required. Please also notify us.

ND0116

The Bible Reading Fellowship

Instruction to your bank or building society to pay by Direct Debit

Please fill in the whole form using a ballpoint pen and send to The Bible Reading Fellowship, 15 The Chambers, Vineyard, Abingdon OX14 3FE.

Service User Number:

5	5	8	2	2	9

Name and full postal address of your bank or building society

To: The Manager	Bank/Building Society
Address	
	Postcode

Name(s) of account holder(s)

Branch sort code

Bank/Building Society account number

Reference

Instruction to your Bank/Building Society

Please pay The Bible Reading Fellowship Direct Debits from the account detailed in this instruction, subject to the safeguards assured by the Direct Debit Guarantee.
I understand that this instruction may remain with The Bible Reading Fellowship and, if so, details will be passed electronically to my bank/building society.

Signature(s)
Date

Banks and Building Societies may not accept Direct Debit instructions for some types of account.

Jan 28th

Feb 11th.
feb. 25th Tea Room
March 3rd
March. 17th Tea Room,
March 31 Anne.

The unforgiving servant | Matt 18 23-35
The wedding feast | Matt 22 1-14
The Ten Maidens oi | Matt 25 1-13 L
(The sheep + Goat) Here.
3 Servants, Matt 25 14-30

April 14. Anne.
~~12~~ April 28. Chris
May   May   June 9th June
                Chris.   23rd
July 7 July 21st